OFFA'S DYKE

A journey in words and pictures

To my late father
Percival Francklin Saunders,
also known as Jim, 1917-2001
and his Voigtlander Bessa 66,
my first real camera.

Published in 2006 by
Gomer Press, Llandysul, Ceredigion, SA44 4JL
www.gomer.co.uk

ISBN 1 84323 699 0

ISBN-13 9781843236993

A CIP record for this title is available from the British Library.

This book is published with the financial support
of the Welsh Books Council.

Printed and bound in Wales at
Gomer Press, Llandysul, Ceredigion

OFFA'S DYKE

A journey in words and pictures

Jim Saunders

Gomer

CONTENTS

Foreword

I consider myself a lucky man indeed to live within close proximity to the wonder that is Offa's Dyke. I share with Jim Saunders a love of the border country and of my native mid-Wales in particular. Some of the beautiful stretches of countryside and waterways which Jim has chosen to highlight in this book are practically on my doorstep. I run with the dogs along the Montgomeryshire Canal, I walk along the banks of the Severn and as a family we often visit Powis Castle and marvel at the ancient oaks in its parkland.

As a Welsh speaker, I might mention Offa's Dyke in general conversation without even thinking about it – the world outside Wales is often referred to as 'beyond Offa's Dyke' or visitors to Wales may be described as having come 'from the other side of Offa's Dyke'. How strange that a piece of engineering built about 1200 years ago should be part of everyday conversation, even for people in west Wales who may have never seen the mighty earthwork itself.

And what a wonder it is – for its sheer size, for the marvellous views to be enjoyed from the ridges and hilltops along its length, and, not least, for the abundance of wildlife which is there for any observant walker to appreciate. As a National Trail, the Offa's Dyke Path is rightly popular with lovers of the countryside, and it's very reassuring to have maps, waymarkers and guides so as to ensure that you make the most of your visit. But in the end, you need a willingness to stop and stare and listen; that will reap rewards wherever you walk.

For the BBC Wales television series, Tessa Dunlop and I had the privilege of tackling the Offa's Dyke Path from south to north, with plenty of stops for tea, banter and debate. We met some marvellous people from all walks of life: farmers, naturalists, artists, historians, ice-cream vendors. And the wildlife? The stunning photographs Jim Saunders took for this book are bound to tempt you to come along and see for yourself.

Iolo Williams

Introduction

So what is this Offa's Dyke? Most people in England and Wales have heard of it but tend to be a little vague about what it actually is, and where to find it. It's a high bank of earth standing next to a wide ditch and, at 1200 years old, it certainly qualifies as an ancient monument. It is also a boundary – the traditional boundary between England and Wales, a psychological and political boundary as well as a physical one. And since 1971, Offa's Dyke has been a walking route too, one of the 15 National Trails of England and Wales.

As an earthwork, Offa's Dyke is in a league of its own. It is really big. Big as in long: about 80 miles (129 km) long, even today. But big as in massive too: even after 1200 years of wind, weather and wear, some parts of the bank stand 25ft above the bottom of the ditch.

Archaeologists love to argue about Offa's Dyke but most agree that it was almost certainly built in the late eighth century AD, probably on the orders of Offa, who was King of Mercia. The kingdom covered the area which we now know as the English Midlands. So far so good. There is less agreement about how and why Offa built his dyke. It seems that it marked the western boundary of his kingdom and that on the far side of it were the Welsh. But was the Dyke supposed to keep the Welsh out? Was the dyke primarily a military structure, built for defence?

Those who take the military view point out that the dyke generally follows high ground so any defender has a military advantage. And if we look at one of the better preserved sections today, it is easy to see that a Saxon standing on the top, looking down into a deep ditch, could certainly make it difficult for anyone to get across without his agreement. And yet, how would you defend a frontier 180 miles long? How would you build an earthwork of this size in the first place without the agreement, or at least the submission, of your neighbours? Wouldn't they try to stop you? Perhaps Offa's Dyke was nothing more than the ultimate status symbol, a statement of power.

Somewhere between these two views lies another possibility – that, like a modern political frontier, Offa's Dyke did allow people and goods to pass to and fro, but in a controlled manner.

It is quite difficult to really capture the sheer scale and significance of this piece of our history. Even from the best viewpoints it is only possible to observe a mile or two of the dyke at one time. The Ordnance Survey map is helpful. Open out Landranger sheet 137 and you can see the dyke stride across the hills between Knighton and Newcastle upon Clun. But if you really want to experience Offa's Dyke in all its glory, and in all its guises, there is only one thing for it: you will have to walk the Offa's Dyke Path.

The Offa's Dyke Path is a long-distance walking route which runs for 177 miles (283km) along the England-Wales border. It connects Chepstow, on the Severn estuary, to Prestatyn, on the north Wales coast. Wherever practicable the path was laid out to follow Offa's Dyke itself, but this does not mean that you will always find the two together. In some places it was not possible to persuade landowners to create new rights of way along the dyke. In others there was simply no dyke to follow. And north of Llangollen, a decision was taken to take the path westward onto the Clwydian Hills, rather than east, to follow the earthwork through the suburbs of Wrexham. This means that when you follow an Offa's Dyke Path fingerpost you will not necessarily be led straight to a piece of the earthwork.

So throughout this book I will always try to make it clear whether I am talking about Offa's Dyke (the earthwork), or the Offa's Dyke Path (the National Trail). And by the end I hope that I will have convinced you that you want to get out among the hills and see the glories of both for yourself.

Chapter I : Lower Wye Valley

The first part of our journey along the Offa's Dyke Path takes us from the Severn estuary, at Sedbury Cliff, to the ancient border town of Monmouth. We travel along the lower Wye valley, designated an Area of Outstanding Natural Beauty. Here we see Offa's Dyke mainly in a woodland setting, but we also have views of the romantic ruins of Tintern Abbey and the opportunity to wander through riverside meadows alongside the Wye itself. In spring, woodland wild flowers are a particular feature of this section of the path, while later in the year, autumn colours provide picture-postcard views.

If you are the kind of person who likes to hold a map the right way up, then you may want start your trip along the Offa's Dyke Path at **Sedbury Cliff**. This is the choice of about two-thirds of the people who walk the path from end to end. They start at Sedbury and walk north, working their way up the map as they go. This tactic has the added advantage that, for most of your journey, sun, wind and rain will be at your back. Not that it ever rains on the Offa's Dyke Path, of course.

On the other hand, if you fancy yourself as a bit of a rebel, or you just like a challenge, there is nothing to stop you starting at the top, at Prestatyn, and working your way down. This is what pioneering archaeologist Sir Cyril Fox did when he surveyed the dyke in the 1920s and '30s. So when Fox arrived at Sedbury Cliff he was at the end of his journey. This is what he wrote at the time:

> The ground falls away steeply to W. and S. as well as vertically to E., thus rendering the position exceptionally dominant; from it practically the whole of the Beachley peninsula is visible, and the eye ranges over wide stretches of sea and land beyond . . . the place seemed to be to an unusual degree characteristic of the Mercian frontier line as a whole and to evoke the very spirit of its creator. On this now silent and deserted spot, at the southern limit of his Mercian dominion, King Offa ought to be commemorated.

Later in the twentieth century, Sedbury Cliff became a bit of a disappointment to southbound walkers, who had been looking forward to a dramatic climax at the end of their holiday. Over the years trees below the cliff had grown up to obscure the view of the Severn Estuary, and encroaching scrub had camouflaged the dyke itself so effectively that its profile was barely visible. But Gloucestershire County Council has worked steadily to improve the situation, to very good effect. Scrub has been steadily cut back year by year, and in 2006 extensive tree surgery on the cliff itself opened up the view again.

Fragrant gorse

The dyke at Sedbury Park

Iolo Williams and Tessa Dunlop at the Pudding Stone, Sedbury Cliff

Chepstow Castle

The end of the Offa's Dyke Path at Sedbury is marked by a large stone set in the top of the dyke, carrying a commemorative plaque. For many years I assumed that this stone had been placed there when the path was opened, as was the case on the seafront at Prestatyn. Now I know that in fact this stone has been there much longer than the National Trail. It is said locally that a horse is buried beneath it. This may be true, but it is interesting to note that a number of other solitary marker stones appear on old Ordnance Survey maps of Sedbury. Perhaps, like the dyke itself, they mark some kind of historic boundary.

One other thing to note about the stone on Sedbury Cliff: if you look at it closely you will see that it contains lots of smaller gravel-sized stones. In fact, it looks rather like an eroded piece of old concrete. This is what geologists call a conglomerate, and this particular conglomerate is known in the Wye valley as Pudding Stone. If you keep you eyes peeled you will find it dotted about in walls, in natural outcrops and just lying about in the woods. It was often used to make millstones.

Shortly after leaving Sedbury Cliff, the Offa's Dyke Path dives into the suburbs of Chepstow. This is not the most attractive part of the path, but it has its points of interest. Look for the row of 1940s council houses built on top of Offa's Dyke in Mercian Way. The name suggests that builders knew that this was an historic site, but did not allow history to interfere with their plans! The view across the river is of magnificent Chepstow Castle.

A castle has stood here for almost a thousand years – they started work on the foundations in 1067, just a year after William the Conqueror invaded. A strategic point for keeping an eye on Wales was clearly one of his priorities. Poet Ivor Waters in his poem entitled 'Chepstow' is clear on the castle's significance:

'Half hidden in oakwoods,
    the portwalls and castle
    built by the Normans
    to hold Gwent in awe.'

Thankfully in a little over a mile we are back in countryside proper, and approaching the woodlands of the lower Wye valley. This section of the National Trail could be said to be atypical. Many parts of the path pass through woodland, but nowhere is it as extensive, or as continuous, as here. These woods have wonderfuly evocative names – Wallhope Grove, Boatwood Plantation, Slip Wood, Quicken Tree Wood, Creeping Hill Wood, Oaken Grove and Highbury Plains.

They are also of considerable historical and ecological interest; according to Dr George Peterken, a woodland conservationist with vast experience, this is one of the most important areas of woodland in the UK. To the layman these woods are obviously picturesque, but the specialist will tell you that they contain a fascinating range of species, both of trees and of wild flowers.

In the spring to early summer you'll see carpets of wood anemone (*Anemone nemorosa*), dog's mercury (*Mercurialis perennis),* and ramsons (*Allium ursinum*), also known as wild garlic. All of these are 'ancient woodland indicators', which means that they grow mainly in woods that are very old – some of the woodland in the lower Wye valley has probably been there since the last Ice Age. Woodland this old is the ecologist's Holy Grail, known in the trade as primary woodland.

But the Wye valley woods have not been by any means static or undisturbed over the last few centuries. Neither has the area always been a picturesque rural idyll. Many of the woods were regularly cropped for timber of various sorts – as far back as the sixteenth century this was a pioneering industrial area (see Digging for History on p. 24), and the Romans mined iron-ore here. The management of woodland was once an industry in its own right, providing the timber and fuel on which other industries depended, notably the early iron industry. Now that all this activity has declined, there are probably more tall trees in the Wye valley today than at any time in the last 2000 years.

This is the ideal habitat for a host of small mammals, bats and birds – ideal terrain also for ornithologist Iolo Williams, who was delighted to spot hawfinches when filming here.

Wild garlic

Creeping Hill wood.

OAK

The fruit of the oak is the acorn and since 1965 a stylised acorn has been used to waymark National Trails in England and Wales. Confusingly, the National Trust also uses a sprig of oak leaves with an acorn as its logo!

Once seasoned (that is, dried), oak is naturally a very hard, strong and durable timber, which means that for centuries it has been used to build timber-framed houses. Before the age of steel it was the raw material of all the Royal Navy's ships. Appropriately, since 1971, it has been used to build stiles, gates and signposts on the Offa's Dyke Path.

NAMES:
English: Common oak
Latin: *Quercus robur*
Welsh: Derwen mes coesynnog

*NATURE FILE * NATURE FILE * NATURE FILE*

Glories of the lower Wye woodland

Among the grandest of the trees to enjoy on this part of the path are two species of oak, the lowland common oak (*Quercus robur*), and the sessile oak (*Quercus petraea*), which is more common in the upland woodlands of Wales. Beech (*Fagus sylvatica*) is native here, but

rarer species such as small-leaved lime (*Tilia cordata*) and wild service tree (*Sorbus torminalis*) are also part of the mix. Then there are pockets of less well-known specialities such as true service tree (*Sorbus domestica*) and English whitebeam (*Sorbus anglica*).

WHAT'S WITH ALL THIS LATIN?

Botanists generally describe plants (including trees) with a Latin name, also called the *scientific* name. The purpose is to overcome the confusion caused when plants have local names which vary from place to place.

A plant's scientific name has two parts. The first states the genus: plants which are closely related are given the same *generic* name. The second part of the name indicates the particular species. Oaks, for example, are of the genus 'Quercus'. So the scientific name of the common (British) oak begins with *Quercus*, to which is added the specific name *robur*, meaning strong or robust. So we have *Quercus robur*, the strong, robust oak.

The sessile oak, which grows in more mountainous areas of Britain, is called *Quercus petraea*, the oak of the rocks.

WHY BADGERS AND DYKES DON'T MIX

Badgers arouse strong feelings – in animal lovers, farmers and archaeologists. In fiction, characters such as Mr Badger in *The Wind in the Willows* conjure up an image of a friendly, harmless animal, living a cosy underground life and minding his own business. Badgers even *look* quite cuddly – something to do with the long striped snout, the thick fur and the little dumpy legs.

I'll admit I have a bit of a soft spot for badgers, but I can tell you that in reality they are not cuddly at all. The real Mr Badger is very strong and heavily built, with long claws (for digging) and a nasty bite if cornered. Even his fur is hard and wiry.

Farmers level three main accusations at badgers: that they spread bovine tuberculosis, that they kill lambs, and that they dig holes in damned inconvenient places.

For archaeologists the last one is the big issue. A badger does like a nice earthwork, and none better than Offa's Dyke. As far as Mr Badger is concerned the dyke is an ideal location to set up home. Because it is a man-made bank, it is relatively easy to dig into. Because it is an ancient monument it is seldom disturbed. It is raised up above the surrounding land, which keeps it nice and dry; and the sloping bank makes for a nice porch from which to study the lie of the land before venturing forth. Where trees grow on the dyke, as they often do, they offer further advantages: shelter from the weather and a handy root system to reinforce the roof of the sett.

When you see a badger sett in Offa's Dyke it is immediately obvious why this is a problem. Badgers shift an awful lot of earth, and they shift it right out from the heart of the dyke. The result is substantial damage to several sections of the earthwork.

It is very difficult to do anything about this. (Believe me, I have tried. For reasons too complicated to go into here I have even been out on the dyke on Christmas Day checking for badger activity.) The problem is that both badgers and ancient monuments are protected by law. So, if a farmer digs up a piece of Offa's Dyke he can be prosecuted. And he can be prosecuted for disturbing a badger sett too. But how do you prosecute a badger for digging up part of the nation's heritage?

Answers on a postcard please.

NAMES: **English:** badger   **Latin:** *Meles meles*   **Welsh:** mochyn daear (lit. earth pig)

Dr George Peterken is a woodland guru. His 1981 book, *Woodland Conservation and Management* (374 pages, £84.00) is the standard text on the subject, read by academics and conservationists everywhere, and it was followed in 1996 by *Natural Woodland*, another substantial tome. So I was delighted when I discovered that this eminent author actually lived amid the woodlands of the Wye valley. When I visited him at home I realised that his house on St Briavels Common is also within 100 metres of the Offa's Dyke Path.

George moved here from Northamptonshire in 1993, but had surveyed the woods of the Wye valley for the Nature Conservancy Council back in 1969. The survey was prompted by the proposal to designate the valley an Area of Outstanding Natural Beauty. At the time, George says, the Wye valley woodlands were almost unknown, and yet his survey found them to be one of the most important areas of woodland in the UK. Today, among his numerous commitments as Associate Professor at Nottingham University and an adviser to the Forestry Commission on nature conservation, George finds time to support community projects which were set up to manage the many flower-rich grasslands of the Wye valley. Neglected fields and orchards have been restored, wild plants and grassland butterflies recorded.

It was appropriate that we should discuss such projects over cappuccinos at the community shop and café in Brockweir, an enterprise that takes sustainability and conservation very seriously. This is a remarkable structure, purpose-built from local oak, roofed with special 'slates' which incorporate solar cells. These generate electricity for the shop, and the heating system is also eco-friendly, using a heat pump to draw warmth from the ground.

I asked George what had particularly drawn him to the Wye valley as a place to live. He used two expressions which I have heard others use when describing the country along the Offa's Dyke Path. 'This is real countryside' and 'Before I came here I didn't know Britain had countryside like this.'

Wood anemone

Community shop, Brockweir.

George Peterken in his own woodland.

Another attraction was that George had the opportunity to own his very own piece of the Wye valley landscape. In addition to nine small fields, which he maintains as flower meadows, he has five acres of the special Wye valley woodland adjacent to his house, where small-leaved lime, beech, sessile oak and pedunculate oak grow with birch, holly, hazel and yew.

From its source high in the mountains of mid-Wales to its mouth at Chepstow (where it meets the Severn) the entire length of the **river Wye** is designated a Site of Special Scientific Interest. It is famous for its salmon, and all along its winding course it passes through an unspoiled rural landscape. But the stretch between Chepstow and Ross-on-Wye is arguably the most scenic. Here the river flows through a steep-sided wooded gorge and passes the famous Symond's Yat Rock, as well as the ancient ruins of Tintern Abbey.

The Offa's Dyke Path crosses the Wye twice, at Monmouth and at Hay-on-Wye, but in the lower Wye valley the National Trail walker also has the option of following the river through the meadows between Brockweir and Bigsweir. The National Trail divides at Brockweir. An upper route follows remnants of Offa's Dyke across St Briavels Common, while the low level alternative hugs the eastern bank of the Wye. Upper and lower routes converge again at Bigsweir Bridge, where a toll house reminds us of how lucrative river-crossing can be for those who manage them. If you want to see both parts of the trail, they make a convenient circuit of 6½ miles (10 km).

One of the best viewpoints over the Wye valley is just off the Offa's Dyke Path at Broadrock, one mile north of Chepstow. This is Wintour's Leap, right beside the B4228. The view from here takes in Piercefield Cliffs, on the opposite bank, and a long curve of the Wye around the Lancaut Peninsula. Mind your step, though; there is a sheer drop in excess of 300 feet (100 m) to the river below. Local legend has it that the name 'Wintour's Leap' comes from Sir John Wintour, a Royalist in the Civil War, who escaped across the river from here when pursued by Parliamentary forces. The site is now popular with climbers and peregrine falcons.

Meadows of the Wye

The Wye from Wintour's Leap

DIGGING INTO HISTORY

Among those who came to admire and record the landscape of the Wye valley at the close of the eighteenth century were the painter J.M.W. Turner and the poet William Wordsworth. Turner painted both Chepstow Castle and Tintern Abbey several times in the early 1790s. Wordsworth penned his poem 'Lines Written a Few Miles above Tintern Abbey' on 13 July 1798.

LEFT: *Tintern Abbey*

CENTRE: *Wye at Bigsweir*

RIGHT: *View from Piercefield House*

oh! how oft,
In darkness, and amid the many shapes
Of joyless day-light; when the fretful stir
Unprofitable, and the fever of the world,
Have hung upon the beatings of my heart,
How oft, in spirit, have I turned to thee
O sylvan Wye!

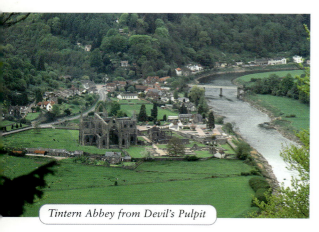

Tintern Abbey from Devil's Pulpit

The Picturesque movement

In the late eighteenth century, the Wye valley became a fashionable destination for followers of the picturesque movement. Enthusiasts of the picturesque saw landscapes as raw material from which pictures could be made. They were particularly keen on rugged, wild-looking scenes, but they also had firm views on what were, and were not, desirable features ('motifs') in a landscape. They were not afraid to make alterations where 'nature' was thought not to measure up.

In 1782 William Gilpin published a book entitled *Observations on the River Wye*, which helped develop this fashion for touring the wilder parts of Britain looking for 'picturesque' scenes to sketch and paint. Gilpin is held by many to have been influential both in the development of tourism in Britain, and in the way in which we look at the landscape today.

Two local advocates of the picturesque were Valentine Morris at Piercefield Park, just north of Chepstow, and the 4th Duke of Beaufort at Tintern Abbey. In the late eighteenth century, Morris laid out walks and created viewpoints with names such as Lover's Leap and the Giant's Cave, which are still marked on the Ordnance Survey map of today. The remains of Piercefield can now be found on the eastern side of Chepstow racecourse, where they look across the Wye to the Offa's Dyke Path at Woodcroft and Broadrock.

timewatch

1067

The foundations for Chepstow Castle were laid, one year after the invasion of William the Conqueror. The architect was another William, a Norman lord called William FitzOsbern

1131

An abbey for Cistercian monks was established at Tintern – the first in Wales. It prospered and buildings were added over the centuries.

1536

Dissolution of the monasteries, including Tintern. Henry VIII seized all the land and wealth it possessed.

1828

Bigsweir Bridge, an iron construction, was erected to carry the road from Monmouth to Chepstow. It ran on the Gloucestershire side of the river until it reached Bigsweir and tolls were collected on the English/Welsh side.

1971

The Wye valley was officially designated an Area of Outstanding Natural Beauty

INDUSTRY IN THE WYE VALLEY

Modern lovers of rural tranquility might be surprised to learn that the eighteenth-century enthusiasts of the picturesque did not see industry as necessarily a blot on the landscape. By that time the Wye valley had already been a hive of industry for centuries. This was industry which grew out of the place, out of the woodlands and out of the rocks beneath them, and it was serviced by the river.

Today the most obvious of these industries is stone quarrying. There are still active limestone quarries in the lower Wye valley; you will probably hear them working as you walk the Offa's Dyke Path.

The Wye valley and the neighbouring Forest of Dean have also been major centres for the mining and refining of metals. Today's sleepy hamlet of Redbrook was once the centre of Britain's copper industry, and there were ironworks at Tintern from the sixteenth to the twentieth centuries. There was even a brass foundry within the ruins of Tintern Abbey itself.

Before the development of the coke-fired blast-furnace in the early eighteenth century, the iron industry was entirely dependent on charcoal as its fuel. The supply of timber above ground, therefore, could be as important in the siting of an ironworks as the availablity of ore below. Arthur Raistrick in his book *Industrial Archaeology* notes that 'as the woods of the south-east [of England] were being steadily depleted, expansion of the [iron] industry in the second century moved to the central Weald . . . and to the Forest of Dean.'

Charcoal was made out in the woods themselves, where wood was carefully stacked and then covered in turf before being set alight to burn very slowly for a period of about two of weeks. The platforms where charcoal was made can still be found not far from the Offa's Dyke Path in, for example, Slip Wood, above Bigsweir.

Before the age of steel hulls, shipbuilding was another industry which required large quantities of timber. So where a good local supply could be found on the banks of a navigable river you could reasonably expect to find shipyards. Sure enough, in the nineteenth century ships were built along the Wye at Monmouth, Brockweir, Chepstow and villages between. These would have included the Wye trow, a boat specially built to navigate the river's often-shallow waters.

*Iolo Williams and Tessa Dunlop
at Bigsweir Bridge*

Boat Inn

The name might make you think otherwise, but the **Devil's Pulpit** is a lovely spot. I have visited it often. Sometimes I have been there on site visits with foresters and archaeologists, to discuss the conservation of the dyke. Often I have come to service the people counter we once had here; but it's tempting enough just to come and take photographs.

The 'Pulpit' itself is a column of bedrock which stands up from the steep hillside, just below Offa's Dyke. It gets its name from a local legend, which says that the Devil would stand at the pulpit to harangue the monks in Tintern Abbey below. There is a splendid view of the abbey, at its best perhaps in spring, when framed by the fresh green foliage of the surrounding trees.

In 1782 William Gilpin was of the opinion that Tintern Abbey could be made more attractive by 'a mallet, judiciously used'. Fortunately, his advice was not followed and in 1901 the abbey was bought by the Crown and the long process of conserving the neglected ruins, now the responsibility of Cadw, was begun.

Don't miss the Boat Inn at **Redbrook** when you are walking the Offa's Dyke Path. As it is on the far side of the river from the National Trail, it is not easily spotted, but it is well worth a visit, whether for the range of real ales served direct from barrels behind the bar, or one of their ploughman's lunches with a huge wedge of Blue Stilton cheese. Whenever I am in the area I try to find an excuse to drop in. Look for the car park and sign just north of the Redbrook's Millennium Green, them take the footpath over the old railway bridge. On a fine day, take your lunch outside and sit at a table overlooking the river. If it is cold or wet, the bar with its old sofa and wood-burning stove could help you while away a very extended lunch-stop, before you turn your sights to the stately town of Monmouth.

Chapter II : The Vale of Usk

The next section of the route takes us from the Wye valley at Monmouth to the edge of the Black Mountains at Pandy. We pass through the Vale of Usk, a quieter, gentler landscape than the steeply-wooded gorge of the Wye. As the English border is left behind, Welsh place-names – or corruptions of Welsh place-names – soon become prevalent. We pass the doors of two thirteenth-century churches and the very impressive 900-year-old White Castle. If you go this way in May you will find some apple blossom, too.

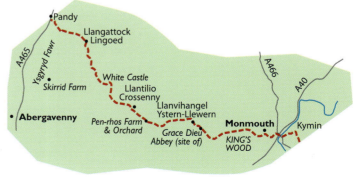

Pill box at Monmouth

Bridge over the Wye

We are first introduced to Monmouth when we reach the Kymin, a National Trust property which offers an excellent view over the town and the countryside of Monmouthshire beyond. On the top of Kymin is the Roundhouse, a very 'picturesque' circular building, painted white, and originally erected as a banqueting house in the late eighteenth century. The Kymin has been a popular place to visit for more than 200 years. A bench just in front of the Roundhouse is well-placed to take in the view, and is popular with National Trail walkers. Close by, and of similar vintage, is the Naval Temple, a rather less pretty construction which commemorates various events and characters in British naval history. Famously, it was visited by Admiral Lord Nelson in 1802.

We descend through woods to enter Monmouth by the Wye Bridge. Note on your right as you approach the bridge a low concrete wall with rectangular slots at about knee height. This is a Second World War 'pillbox' (gun emplacement) built, presumably, to protect the river crossing. Earlier in our journey we were close to another, which stands, or rather sits, in a field at the western end of Bigsweir Bridge.

Monmouth is not a very big town, but it is the largest we will pass through before Prestatyn at the northern end of the path. Its English name comes from the river Monnow, which meets the Wye just below the town. In Welsh it is Trefynwy, literally Monnow Town. The Monnow curls around the town on the west and south sides, while on the east is the Wye, giving Monmouth a naturally strong defensive position. Like many of the border towns, Monmouth has a long history, dating back at least to Norman times. King Henry V, victor at the Battle of Agincourt, was born here and is commemorated in Agincourt Square.

The Offa's Dyke Path follows the broad and attractive Monnow Street from Agincourt Square down to the historic Monnow Bridge, with its built-in gatehouse. Here we leave the town proper and find our way to Watery Lane, leading back to the countryside and to the leafy expanse of King's Wood.

Beyond King's Wood, and close by the path, is the site where Grace Dieu Abbey once stood. Grace Dieu was a Cistercian house, like Tintern in the Wye valley, and Llanthony Priory, further north. However, unlike these two famous ruins Grace Dieu leaves little mark on the landscape today. It is commemorated in the names of Abbey Meadow, through which the Offa's Dyke Path passes and Abbey Bridge, by which the National Trail crosses the river Trothy (afon Troddi).

And here we come to our first seriously Welsh place-name. Many visitors to Wales have difficulty with the place-names, not least because so many begin with 'Llan', which most English speakers cannot even pronounce. Well, this section of the Offa's Dyke Path is a bit of an assault course for such unfortunate innocents.

Our route takes us through the villages with the anglicised names of Llanvihangel-Ystern-Llewern, Llantilio Crossenny and Llangattock Lingoed. We also pass close by Llanvetherine and Llanfihangel Crucorney. But bear in mind that the correct name of Llanvihangel-Ystern-Llewern is Llanfihangel Ystum Llywern, Llantilio Crossenny is Llandeilo Gresynni and Llangattog Lingoed is Llangatwg Lingoed; and, by the way, Llanvetherine is an anglicised version of Llanwytherin! I confess that even after 18 years as Offa's Dyke Path Officer I sometimes found it difficult to remember which was which of these villages.

However, learning just a few words of Welsh can make place-names easier to understand and remember. And the first thing to learn is that 'Llan' is a word for church or enclosure; the second part of a name often refers to the dedication of the church in that village or town. So the church at Llangollen is dedicated to St Collen. At Llandrindod Wells we find the church of the Holy Trinity (Trindod). So the next trick then is to learn the Welsh names of a few popular saints. Mary, for example, is 'Mair', from which we get Llanfair. (The substitution of an 'f' for the 'm', is called a mutation. I won't go into that here. I tried to explain Welsh mutations once before in print, and got into all sorts of trouble.)

A bilingual welcome

Cow parsley

So, Llanfihangel-Ystern-Llywern? Mihangel is the Welsh for Michael. Is the village church dedicated to St Michael? Why don't you take a look? We will be passing through the churchyard. But to give you a little encouragement I can tell you that the church at Llantilio Crossenny is St Teilo's – and a fine one it is, too – and that at Llangattock Lingoed it is St Cadoc's.

I won't pretend that it is easy to work out all Welsh place-names, nor English place-names for that matter. In Welsh, mutations which change the first letter of words make it difficult even to look them up in a dictionary. And when you are close to the English border, names are often mangled. They may be half English and half Welsh, as at Bettws Dingle, near Hay-on-Wye; and Llanfair Waterdine, near Knighton. Of course most of the border towns have both an English and a Welsh name. Chepstow is Cas-gwent, Hay-on-Wye is Y Gelli Gandryll. Less well-known is that many towns which have been English for centuries have Welsh names too. Shrewsbury is Amwythig, Hereford is Henffordd, and Cambridge is Caergrawnt. Welsh is still in everyday use in much of Wales – to hear it you need only tune into BBC Radio Cymru!

Just before Llantilio Crossenny the Offa's Dyke Path passes through the cider orchards of Pen-rhos Farm. Although the path passes close to the cider-growing county of Herefordshire this is the only extensive area of orchard on the National Trail, and it is in Monmouthshire. It is, however, owned and managed by the long-established Hereford firm of Bulmers. These particular orchards were planted in 1997. Pen-rhos Farm had been a typical mixed livestock farm with sheep, and both dairy and beef cattle. It was farmed by two brothers who had no heirs, so when they retired in their late seventies they sold to Bulmers.

Farm Manager Alan Williams came to Pen-rhos Farm from another Bulmers holding, at Monnington-on-Wye in Herefordshire. He now looks after 169 hectares of well-established orchards, with six other full-time staff. These include Jennifer Lovering, who milked cattle on the farm before Bulmers took over, and stayed on to work for the new owners.

ON NATURE'S TRAIL

Plants to torment walkers

There are many attractive wild plants along the Offa's Dyke Path but there are are also some which walkers might prefer to do without.

Bramble (*Rubus fruticosus)* is a hugely variable plant with as many as 1,000 sub-species. But most walkers know brambles when they see them. For one thing they are very prickly. For another they have a cunning habit of trailing across a path just above the ground so that they can wrap themselves around innocent ankles/trip innocent passers-by. They are particularly fond of woolly socks and will form an intimate bond with them at the drop of a hat. But if no socks are to be had they will be just as happy to draw a little blood from an exposed ankle.

Brambles can grow at an impressive rate and their ability to root wherever they touch soil means that they can form an impenetrable thicket surprisingly quickly. Still, without brambles there would be no blackberries; and what would September be without blackberrying?

Thistle is another prickly customer, though much less of a nuisance to walkers than brambles. Several species of thistle grow in the UK. Pictured here are two which grow together alongside Offa's Dyke on Cwm Sanaham hill: marsh thistle *Cirsium palustre* and spear thistle *Cirsium vulgare*. Spear thistle is the archetypal Scottish thistle, with spiny bulbous head topped by a brush of lilac 'florets'. Just occasionally one comes across a neglected pasture where thistles grow so thickly that it can be difficult to fight a way through. But the main nuisance value of thistles, as far as walkers are concerned, is their habit of waiting inconspicuously on grassy banks for someone to sit down to take in the view.

Stinging Nettle

No introduction needed. Once you have encountered stinging nettles you are unlikely to forget them – you only have to brush against one to get a painful sting. And this is easily done because stinging nettles are fairly inconspicuous, lurking around the base of stiles and in among other green foliage. The Latin name gives doctors the word 'urticaria', a general term for any skin rash like that caused by nettle stings. The phrase 'grasp the nettle', comes from the traditional belief that if you squeeze a nettle firmly, the stinging hairs will be crushed and you will not be hurt. Hmm.

NAMES:
English: Stinging nettle
Latin: *Urtica dioica*
Welsh: Danadl poethion

NATURE FILE * NATURE FILE * NATURE FILE *

BATS AND BUZZARDS

We cannot go much further in our journey without mentioning, or indeed seeing, a buzzard. If you asked me to name a bird which typifies the Offa's Dyke Path this would be it. Beautiful, graceful birds which can be seen soaring, wings outstretched, just about anywhere along the National Trail. When you first see one you may well think it is a small eagle. Buzzards often perch on roadside telegraph poles too, but will drop and glide away if you stop to take a closer look, often teasing you by landing again on the next pole along.

When I first came to the Marches the buzzards were a real treat. After twenty years of seeing one almost every day I still look up when I hear their mewing call. I do the same when I hear crows calling angrily, because crows habitually attack, or 'mob' buzzards. Most recently I saw this happen right over my back garden in the middle of Knighton.

Buzzards are unmistakeably birds of prey, and are said to hunt rabbits; but if a dull-witted pheasant strays into the path of an oncoming car (which they often do) a buzzard will not pass up the opportunity for a free meal. So you will occasionally see one lazily flap up from a heap of feathers in the middle of a road too. Perhaps this is why crows dislike them so much.

For night-time fliers, possibly the churchyard of St Cadoc's is the place to be. They are very proud at Llangattock Lingoed that lesser horseshoe bats have made their home in the roofspace of the church.

The roofspace at St. Cadoc's provides an ideal maternity roost for a colony of **Lesser Horseshoe bats**. This **rare** bat, about the size of a plum, can be seen emerging from the building through the summer months, about half an hour after sunset and again at dawn. They catch flies and moths in the air and can pick insects off stones and branches, finding their prey in the dark by use of ultrasound and a well developed echolocation system. There are 16 resident bat species in Britain all protected by Law.

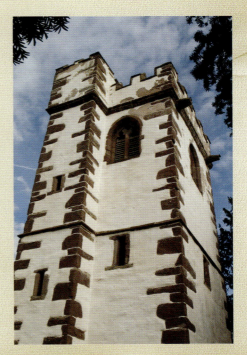

NAMES:	**English:** buzzard	**Latin:** *Buteo buteo*	**Welsh:** bwncath
NAMES:	**English:** lesser horseshoe bat	**Latin:** *Rhinolophus hipposideros*	**Welsh:** ystlum pedol lleiaf

I visited in late May and sadly the apple blossom was just over, but I learned a lot: for example that cider is typically made with a mixture of juices from a range of apples. There are 'bittersweet', 'sharp' and 'bittersharp' cider apples, but sweet juice from cooking and eating apples is often used too. 'Bittersweet' apples contain all-important tannin, which gives dry cider a distinctive taste.

Alan reeled off a list of varieties of apple grown at Pen-rhos Farm: Debinett, Harry Masters Jersey, Michelin (yes, they are French), Yarlington Mill, Ashton Bitter, Tremlettes Bitter, Katy, Somerset Red Streak and Ellis Bitter. All of these end up at the Bulmers works in Hereford. Apparently Bulmers buy more than 40% of the apples grown in England and Wales.

Alan and his workers do not just have to tend to the apple trees: the grass which grows between them is important too. The crop is harvested by mechanically shaking the tree until the apples fall to the ground; and then gathering them up with a tractor-mounted harvester. The rôle of the turf is, of course, to make sure that the apples have a soft landing and do not bruise. More important, it provides a tough, dense surface which harvesting machines can traverse without causing damage to the soil. This in turn allows apples to be picked up clean. Harvesting begins with the Katy apples in early September and ends in late November, with the Debinetts and Yarlington Mills.

The church of St. Teilo at Llantilio Crossenny is a couple of hundred yards off the Offa's Dyke Path, but it is worth a visit if you have some time in hand. The spire is quite unusual: at first it appears to be clad in slate, which would be nothing to remark upon, but closer examination shows that roof is in fact of wooden tiles or 'shingles'. In the chancel there are a number of interesting memorial slabs laid in the floor. One, dating from the 1600s, depicts an adult couple and three smaller male figures, all in distinctive Elizabethan-style costume. According to the church guide these are believed to be Jane and John Walderne who died in 1620, and their three sons. Does this mean that the sons died as children?

A juicy crop

St Teilo's church

DIGGING INTO HISTORY

The White Castle

'Its isolation, and the effect it gives of remaining much as it was when first built, make the White Castle exceptional even among the always romantic castles of Wales.'

The Shell Guide to Wales

Just beyond Llantilio Crossenny the Offa's Dyke Path climbs a gently sloping lane to the gate of the White Castle. It then loops around the perimeter of the castle, making an almost-complete circuit of the moat. So the walker gets a good view of the massive curtain wall and of the moat, which is still full of water more than 800 years after the castle was built. The name 'White Castle' is believed to derive from the fact that the stonework was once covered with lime mortar. The castle is under the care of Cadw, the historic monuments agency for Wales, and is open to the public – so give yourself the time to go in and take a proper look.

Historians talk of the White Castle as one of a set of three, known as 'the trilateral', the other two being Grosmont (y Grysmwnt) and Skenfrith (Ynysgyrwraidd). Skenfrith is about 5 miles north-east of White Castle, Grosmont a similar distance north-north-east, so that on the map the three mark out an almost equilateral triangle. All were originally built in the twelfth century, by the Normans, consolidating their territorial gains in this part of south Wales. For a while in the thirteenth century, when this area was very much in contention, these castles became strategically very important, and this was the case again in the fifteenth century when Grosmont was held by the Welsh forces of Owain Glyndŵr, but was then lost to the English under their future King Henry.

1201

Three royal castles were granted by King John to Hubert de Burgh – White Castle, Grosmont and Skenfrith. He undertook major rebuilding work of the Norman strongholds.

1387

King Henry V was born in Monmouth. He governed England from 1413 to 1422 and in 1420 was made heir and regent of France as well, when he married Catherine, daughter of the King of France.

1680

Ysgyryd Fawr (also known as St Michael's Mount) was used as a favourite meeting-place for Catholics – at a time when it was unsafe for them to practise their religion openly.

1794

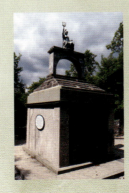

Local gentry in Monmouth raised 80 guineas to build a banqueting house at Kymin so that they would remain dry at their favourite picnic site whatever the weather. For the price of one shilling and 6 pence, a group of people could feast inside at a table covered with 'a fresh white table cloth'.

NATURE AND INDUSTRY AT PANDY

Spot teasels growing anywhere near Pandy and you will be reminded of their importance to the industry that once flourished here. These tall, distinctive plants were useful because of the spiny, egg-shaped flower heads. The spines end in tiny hooks, and it was this prickly characteristic which gave the teasel an important rôle in fulling mills such as that at Pandy. Arthur Raistrick in his book *Industrial Archaeology* explains this better than I can:

> In the mid sixteenth century another process of cloth finishing was part mechanised and transferred to the fulling mill – the raising of the nap on cloth. This had been done with teasels fixed on a hand frame with which the cloth was brushed. The gig-mill was a large drum with frames of teasels covering it and revolved from the same shaft and wheel as the stocks, so that later fulling-mills may contain traces or remains of a gig-mill.

Teasel for teasing, sloes for dyeing.

Incidentally, the word 'teasel' relates to wool as well – teasels were used by hand-weavers to *tease out* wool prior to spinning. And the Welsh name commonly used was *cribau'r pannwr*, literally 'fuller's combs'.

There were numerous fulling-mills in Wales before the larger woollen mills took over in earnest in the latter half of the nineteenth century, so the name Pandy is a common one. This particular one was home to John Davies, local Calvinistic minister, author and historian who assisted Sir Joseph Bradbury in his compiling of the authoritative work, *The History of Monmouthshire*.

The former fulling-mill, now a bunkhouse

One of the treasures of Llangattock Lingoed

Teasel, once vital to the fulling process

To visit the church of St Cadoc at **Llangattock Lingoed** we only need deviate a few paces from our route, which passes right through the churchyard. I happened by here in May 2003 and found the church covered in scaffolding and shrouded in polythene. The stone-tiled roof of the nave had been found to be in danger of imminent collapse, so an urgent major restoration was under way. During the works numerous interesting discoveries were made about the fabric of the church, including the inevitable woodworm and death-watch beetle. Most exciting though, was a huge wall-painting of St George and the Dragon, dating from the 1400s. Drop in and have a look, the church is open every day. The render on the tower is a traditional lime (not cement) mortar, and was considered by the restorers as the best way to protect the stonework from further decay.

Pandy – the Welsh for 'fulling-mill, which is a good clue to its history – is a small hamlet beside the main Hereford to Abergavenny road, but its name looms large in any itinerary of the Offa's Dyke Path. It is the last stop before the path climbs onto the top of the Black Mountains, where it remains for more than 15 miles. So the long-distance walker has to make a decision at Pandy: either to stop here for the night and then try to make for Hay-on-Wye – 17 miles, mostly above 1,700 feet (500 metres) – next day; or to break the journey somewhere along the mountain ridge. There are not many opportunities to do the latter, and all involve descending into the valley on one side or other of the ridge, and then climbing back up in the morning. Groups who stay at the Black Mountain Lodge (a roomy bunkhouse in what was once the fulling-mill) can only imagine the noise and activity of years gone by as raw cloth was beaten and cleansed by running water.

Chapter III : The Hatterrall Ridge

And so to the Black Mountains, one of the more challenging sections of the National Trail, where the path rises to over 2,100 ft (650 m). If you pick the right day you will have spectacular views in all directions. To the east you will be looking over the hedges and fields of Herefordshire, to the west into the mountains of Wales, with the romantic ruins of Llanthony Priory just below. The path surface here varies from soft turf to wet peat, with stone slabs on the more fragile sections. The vegetation is typical of high moorland: heather, bracken, bilberry and cotton grass. Be prepared for any kind of weather!

Lane to Hatterrall Hill

A view of England

I have been up on the Hatterrall Ridge in all weathers: in scorching sun (which gave one of my companions sunstroke), in snow storms and in a howling gale which made it difficult to stand. All these outings were very exciting and memorable, but they could equally have been very unpleasant if I had not had the right clothing for the conditions. Hence the hardened walker's mantra: 'There is no such thing as bad weather; only inappropriate clothing.'

To reach the Hatterrall Ridge from Pandy, first cross the river Honddu by a footbridge in a belt of trees, then the Hereford to Newport railway line by a pedestrian level-crossing. After a climb through lanes, you come to a five-bar gate leading to the open hill. This is Hatterrall Hill proper, though the name tends to be applied to the whole of the ridge north from here. After a couple of hundred yards the path passes through an Iron Age hill-fort. This one is no Maiden Castle, and there are more impressive examples further north, in the Clwydian Hills, but it is a feature worth noticing.

The path continues to climb. It does not drop below 1,500 ft (480 m) for the next 12 miles and walkers will not encounter any habitation, shelter or road crossings in that distance. It is a grand walk, though. On a fine summer's day you can look east across the patchwork fields of Herefordshire to the Malvern Hills and the Cotswolds beyond. To the west, layer upon layer of mountain ridges spread into the distance, while below, in the shelter of the Vale of Ewyas, are the almost absurdly romantic ruins of Llanthony Priory.

The Hatterrall Ridge is the last bastion of the Black Mountains, looming over the lowlands of Herefordshire to the east. As well as carrying the Offa's Dyke Path, the crest of the ridge marks the boundary of the Brecon Beacons National Park and the border between England and Wales. The eastern flank of the ridge, along with the spur of the Black Hill, have a very Welsh aspect but are actually in England. The National Trail, as it meanders along the ridge, crosses in and out of England several times.

It is on the Hatterrall Ridge that the northbound walker on the Offa's Dyke Path first encounters peat. I studied Soil Science a little (as little as possible, actually) in my youth, so I can tell you with authority that for the most part it is best left to boffins and gardeners. However, peat is one soil type which is very easy to recognise. Peat is soft, black, and often very, very, wet.

Because they are so susceptible to erosion, peat soils are particularly problematic for path managers. So we can consider ourselves lucky that there is not very much peat on the Offa's Dyke Path, and that where is does occur it is not very deep. Two 'problem areas' have been known for many years: the northern end of the Hatterrall Ridge, and the moorland plateau of Cyrn y Brain, just beyond Llangollen. Extensive works have been carried out over a number of years to protect the moorland vegetation, and the peat beneath it, at both of these sites. At Cyrn y Brain a raised walkway has been made from railway sleepers. On the Hatterrall Ridge and Hay Bluff various techniques have been employed, but probably the most successful has been the laying of large stone slabs to form a continuous path through the more vulnerable areas of peat. In both cases the objective has been to give walkers an easy surface to walk on, which they would naturally choose to follow, so that the vegetation on either side is protected. On Cyrn y Brain, vegetation has returned up to the very edges of the walkway. The work on Hatterrall Ridge has been more recent, but there are already signs of recovery.

This kind of intervention is always controversial, though. Many people object to 'unnatural' surfaces on footpaths, especially in the remote uplands, and on Hatterrall Ridge both farmers and walkers had to be persuaded that this was a good idea. There is, in fact, a general reluctance to introduce artificial surfacing on the Offa's Dyke Path, and indeed, for the most part, the surface of the National Trail is wearing well. Hard surfacing is very much a remedy of last resort.

Walkway of stone

Descending Hay Bluff

Mike Scruby is the outdoor type. Indeed, he is what many people would regard as the archetypal outdoor type: a National Park warden. He works for the Brecon Beacons National Park Authority, and his official title is actually Area Manager East. That doesn't quite have the same ring though, does it?

Mike has been the man in overall charge of the conservation and surfacing works on the Offa's Dyke Path in the Black Mountains for many years and I have known and worked with him since he joined the National Park 14 years ago, originally as warden for the Northern Scarp of the Black Mountains. Before that he worked for the National Trust and the Avon Wildlife Trust, so caring for the environment has always been at the heart of his work.

Mike studied geology at university, a fact which came in useful (to me) a few years ago when I received an e-mail from a student in China seeking help with a study of sandstone landforms. Knowing that the Black Mountains are made of sandstone, I was happy to pass the enquiry on swiftly to a trained geologist. He was pleased, too, as you can imagine.

In preparation for writing this book I arranged to meet Mike in Hay-on-Wye, and yes, it was during the week of the great literary festival, so it was packed. We drove up to the common below Hay Bluff, where there is a small informal car park, next to the site of a stone circle, and were only too glad to take off on a short circular walk. It was a magnificent May afternoon, with blue skies and a (very) fresh breeze.

We climbed the eastern flank of the Bluff on the Offa's Dyke Path to reach the ridge near Llech y Lladron (the robber's stone). Then we turned right, and walked along the top to the trig. point (triangulation pillar) on the Bluff, before descending the steep scarp slope back to the car park. While I took off my boots, Mike went off to chat to the ice cream vendor – and just then, who should pull up alongside me in a large BMW but the comedian Jeremy Hardy. Strange things happen in Hay.

Winter in the Black Mountains

Mike Scruby

Peat moors

NAMES:
English: Hare's tail cottongrass
Latin: *Eriophorum vaginatum*
Welsh: Plu'r gweunydd unben
(lit. moorland feathers)

Peat soil forms in places where there is high rainfall and/or poor drainage. It is made up of the blackened remains of partly decomposed plants which have been prevented from breaking down completely because of waterlogging. In Britain, peat is most often found in the uplands of the north and west, where rainfall is high, and conversely, in the low, flat fens of eastern England, where, before man's intervention, drainage was naturally poor.

Upland peat soils usually become very acid, so that only a small range of plants can grow on them. Easily-spotted are the cotton grasses *Eriophorum vaginatum* and *Eriophorum angustifolium* (strictly speaking not true grasses, but sedges) and the thick spongy sphagnum moss. In the drier parts heather (*Calluna vulgaris* and *Erica spp*) and bilberry (*Vaccinium myrtillus*) will be found.

Plants grow slowly in peat, particularly at high altitudes as on Hatterrall Ridge, and, if damaged, they take a long time to recover. When they do not, the soft peat itself is exposed, making a surface which is difficult to walk on and very easily eroded. In wet weather it turns to a fine black slurry which is washed away and in dry weather it turns to dust which the wind picks up and carries off. As walkers travail patches of exposed peat the path gradually widens, and the erosion spreads too.

Careless burning of heather is another danger. When dry, peat catches light easily, and fires in deep peat can burn for weeks.

BILBERRY and HEATHER

Heather has always been useful to countryside dwellers and Britain actually has 75% of the world's resource of open heather moorland. After the Second World War over-grazing, forestry plantation and the spread of bracken became a serious threat. More recently, many projects have promoted the conservation of heather moorland. Historically, heather was used as thatching material, bedding, packing and all manner of medicinal remedies – hot poultices to treat chilblains, liniment for rheumatism and gout, infusions for coughs colds and cystitis. Bilberry pie, anyone? Picking enough bilberries for a pie is a job only for the very patient walker. The berries are small (4mm across) but delicious in a very small pie. They ripen in August.

NATURE FILE * NATURE FILE * NATURE FILE *

RAVENS

Another thing to look out for in the Black Mountains is the jet-black raven, the largest member of the crow family. The raven is a bird of hills and cliffs, and you may see it anywhere along the Offa's Dyke Path; but in my mind it is particularly associated with this area.

The differences between a raven, a rook and a crow, are not immediately obvious, particularly as you will usually see them in flight quite high above you. All three are large all-black birds. Bird books tell you that the raven has a longer neck and head, which is supposed to make it look like a Maltese Cross. I have never quite been able to see that. The first I am aware of a raven is usually when I hear a very deep 'craaak' overhead.

If you do spot one or more ravens, stop and watch them for a while and you may be treated to a display of raven aerobatics. One of the ravens' favourite tricks is to fold his wings and roll briefly onto his back. On a windy spring day this looks like sheer exuberance. It's no wonder that Iolo Williams so admires them: 'If I came back to Earth as a bird, I could do far worse than returning as a raven. They are one of the few birds that appear to fly because they can and because they enjoy it.'

Seen close up the raven can look quite frightening. It has a very stout beak which looks as though it might have evolved for cracking nuts, or fingers. No wonder then that in folklore the raven is an omen of evil or death.

> 'The raven himself is hoarse,
> That croaks the fatal entrance of Duncan
> Under my battlements'
>
> *Macbeth*

But the raven can be associated with beauty, and with security, too. Hence we have 'raven-haired beauty' to describe a woman with lustrous black hair. And the famous ravens of the Tower of London, according to legend, guarantee the safety of the kingdom.

TOP: *Ravens in flight*

CENTRE: *Iolo Williams and Tessa Dunlop watch the aerobatics*

BOTTOM: *Queen of the May, Green Man Festival at Clun*

NAMES: **English:** raven **Latin:** *Corvus corax* **Welsh:** cigfran (lit. meat-crow)

Hay Bluff and the **Hatterrall Ridge** are common land. In the past this term caused some confusion, and there was a popular misconception that commons were publicly owned, or that the general public had always had a right of free access to them. The Countryside and Rights of Way Act of 2000 did, in fact, introduce the 'Right to Roam', so that much common land is now open to the public. Historically, though, the term 'common' referred to access for grazing and various other agricultural or economic activities, rather than recreation. Typically, a piece of common might be owned by a large estate but grazed by a number of neighbouring farmers. Each farm or farmer would be legally entitled to release a specified number of animals on to the common. This is the arrangement on the Hatterrall Ridge, with the interesting twist that one of the major landowners is now the Brecon Beacons National Park.

It is notoriously difficult to police the grazing of common land, and the result can be overgrazing. Some ecologists will tell you that this has been a major cause of damage to moorland vegetation and loss of biodiversity, and Iolo Williams once referred to sheep as nothing more than 'woolly maggots'. When I was a student in the 1970s the overgrazing of commons was used as the classic example of a whole range of environmental problems – ranging from air pollution to overfishing – where a shared resource was being damaged by competing individuals, companies or nations. A famous article, 'The Tragedy of the Commons' by Garrett Hardin, had appeared in the American journal *Science* in 1968, and generated much discussion among environmentalists and economists.

However, Mike Scruby tells me that when he last met the Hay Bluff Commoners they were complaining that hill farming is now in such a poor state that they may soon take their stock off the hill altogether. From a scientific point of view it would certainly be very interesting to observe the results if this were to happen.

Grazing on common land

Foal and mare on Hay Bluff

DIGGING INTO HISTORY

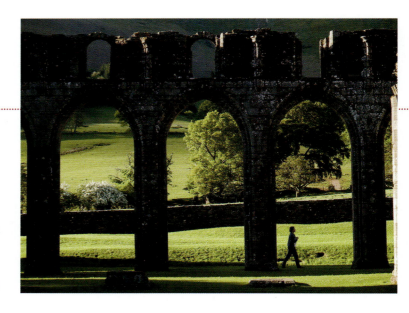

Llanthony Priory

The Llanthony Priory pictured here is the first of three to take the name. It is about as romantic a ruin as you could wish to find, tucked away in the Vale of Ewyas, surrounded by the Black Mountains, accessible only by one narrow winding road, and it is nearly 900 years old. You will not be at all surprised to learn that JMW Turner painted here in the same period that he visited Tintern Abbey and Chepstow Castle.

This priory was built in the early 1100s by the Cistercians, an order that took the simple life very seriously; so much so that they refused to wear underwear or even to dye their tunics black, as other monks did. Either practice they considered decadent, and contrary to monastic teaching. So they wore undyed woollen garments next to their skin, day and night, and became known as the White Monks.

Seeking solitude and isolation, the Cistercians chose remote, rural places for their monasteries, each of which had to be self-sufficient. But despite the frugal existence of the monks, Cistercian abbeys became big landowners and farmers, and their influence was considerable. They even did their bit for industry: mining, quarrying, processing the products of their farms, and manufacturing pottery.

The medieval Cistercians forged close links with Welsh princes and their monasteries became centres for Welsh literature.

Llanthony number two was Llanthony Secunda, founded in 1136 near Gloucester. Opinions seem to differ as to whether this was intended to be just a subsidiary of the original, or whether the monks chose to move to the English lowlands in search of an easier life. Today the two sites could not be more different. I came across Llanthony Secunda quite by chance once, when trying to find my way around the industrial outskirts of Gloucester. It looked sadly out of place.

The third Llanthony, Llanthony Tertia, was a nineteenth-century invention, just up the valley, at Capel-y-ffin. It was part of a short-lived attempt to revive the monastic way of life.

I took the pictures here in late May, on an evening when sun gave the ruins a warm glow and all around was spring blossom and fresh green foliage. A family had just arrived on half-term holiday, staying at a neighbouring property. They were thrilled with the place.

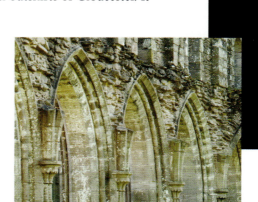

1100

Cistercians began work on the first Llanthony Priory in the heart of the Black Mountains. Tradition has it that Saint David himself had lived in this valley for a time, in the age of the saints. The Church of Saint David at Llanthony, therefore, carries on a tradition of worship and prayer which may go back much earlier than the priory. Fittingly, the altar in the church is aligned so that it points to the rising sun on March 1st, St David's Day.

1762

The Church of St Mary was built at Capel-y-ffin in 1762, replacing an earlier chapel of which nothing remains. The porch was added in 1817. It is still in the tradition of a chapel-of-ease – a small building of whitewashed stone with a wooden turret and one bell.

1925

Eric Gill at Capel-y-ffin developed typefaces such as Perpetua, used on Offa's Dyke Path signs.

1927

Poet David Jones at Capel-y-ffin began work on In Parenthesis, a collection shaped by his experiences as a foot soldier in the Royal Welsh Fusiliers during the First World War.

1957

Capel-y-ffin Youth Hostel opened its doors to travellers.

The Bronze Age in the Black Mountains

Four thousand years before the Offa's Dyke Path came this way, there were people walking, working and living on the Hatterrall Ridge.

This was the Bronze Age, around 2,000 years BC, and archaeologists believe that the climate was warmer and drier then. There may even have been arable farming on the top of Hatterrall Ridge. Archaeologist Peter Dorling tells me that evidence of this has been found at similar altitudes in the Brecon Beacons. The cooler, wetter conditions which gave rise to the formation of peat soils did not really take hold until about 1400 BC.

Numerous flints have been found on Hatterrall Ridge. Now flint is not a local material – it is normally associated with the Chalk downs of south and east England – so its presence here suggests that people on the ridge came from afar, or traded with far-off places. Furthermore, these flints are more than just arrowheads: there are small flakes, too, such as would be produced by the manufacture of flint tools. This in turn suggests that Bronze Age people did not only hunt up here, but actually lived and worked on the ridge.

There are Bronze Age burial cairns dotted along Hatterrall Ridge right up to Hay Bluff. They are barely visible today, and at one time the Offa's Dyke Path went right through the middle of one, until Peter asked for it to be diverted.

Flint arrowhead

Three miles up the Vale of Ewyas from Tintern is **Capel-y-ffin.** Hardly a place at all, really; more a scatter of farms and cottages around the tiny stone-roofed church of St Mary the Virgin. It is marked on the map, though, and does have one or two claims to fame.

One of these is Capel-y-ffin Youth Hostel, a real old-fashioned country hostel, offering cheap accommodation with basic facilities, faithful to the spirit of the early youth hostellers. The hostel opened in its present location, a former hill farm, in 1958. Paula Slack, joint warden with her partner Paul Phillips (yes really, Paul and Paula) tells me that there had previously been a hostel at the old monastery, just down the road.

I spent a weekend at Capel-y-ffin Youth Hostel in the early 1990s with a group of volunteers from the Offa's Dyke Association. It wasn't particularly warm, as I recollect, but had loads of atmosphere. When you stayed at Capel-y-ffin you knew you were in the country. There is a footpath down to the valley from the ridge, via The Vision farm. Sadly Capel-y-ffin hostel is scheduled for closure in September 2007.

St Mary's church is worth a visit if only to see the extraordinary collection of ancient yew trees which line the churchyard. Many country churchyards have an ageing yew or two, but I have never seen such an impressive group of huge trees gathered in one place. If you want to attend a service at St Mary's you will need to plan your trip carefully; there are just two services a month, both in the afternoon: mass at 2.30pm on the first Sunday and evensong at 2.30pm on the third.

Artist and designer Eric Gill set up a religious community at Capel-y-ffin when he bought part of the former monastery of Llanthony Tertia in 1924. Among other things he designed typefaces, including the well-known Gill Sans, which is still in use on modern computers, including mine. Coincidentally, his Perpetua Bold was used on the original oak signs for the Offa's Dyke Path, Pennine Way and other National Trails. One other notable member of the community at Capel-y-ffin was artist and poet David Jones, a great friend of Eric Gill.

Postbox at Capel-y-ffin

St Mary's Church

Chapter IV : Hay to Knighton

At Hay we cross the Wye again, then we travel on to the towns of Kington and Knighton. These are three archetypal border market towns, right on the edge of Wales, nestling among hills and linked by the Offa's Dyke Path.

Our route continues up hill and down dale, dipping in and out of England. Just north of Kington we are reunited with Offa's Dyke itself, for the first time since Monmouth, and say goodbye to Herefordshire. Wildlife on ridges and riverbanks, hilltops and hedgerows will delight walkers at any time of year.

Buskers at the Hay Festival

At the Castle Bookshop

Hay-on-Wye is a very literary town. For decades it has promoted itself as 'The Town of Books', where every other shop is a bookshop, and even the castle and cinema have been turned over to the book trade. Since 1987 Hay has also been home to the Hay Festival, which takes over the town each year in the last week of May. This has grown and grown and is now one of the major international literary festivals. It has even spawned offspring overseas, in Segovia, Spain, and in Cartagena, Colombia.

When the festival is on you just don't know who you will bump into in Hay. In 2006 I went along to see the evolutionary biologist Steve Jones, former US Vice-president Al Gore, and Welsh poets Christine Evans and Nigel Jenkins. Generally milling about the festival site I spotted journalist Rosie Boycott, documentary-maker Nick Broomfield and the writer Jeanette Winterson. On the way to the toilets I met a woman carrying a very appealing chocolate-coloured puppy. So pretty was he that I did not notice at first that she was the actress Jemma Redgrave.

Twenty-five years ago, before the days of the Hay Festival, you might have come across writer Bruce Chatwin wandering the streets of Hay or, more likely, the hills around. His novel *On the Black Hill* was set in the border country of Radnorshire and Herefordshire, on a farm called The Vision, near a fictional town called Rhulen. It was made into a film in 1987, with a spectacular opening sequence of the Hatterrall Ridge from the air. Rhulen seems to be a thinly-disguised Hay and many of the other place-names featured can be found locally, though not necessarily as set out in the book. The real Black Hill (also known as the Cat's Back) is a spur jutting into Herefordshire from the northern end of Hatterrall Ridge; there is a Vision Farm just below the Offa's Dyke Path, near Capel-y-ffin, and a smallholding called Cockalofty – on the common just below Hay Bluff – also shares its name with a farm in the book.

One person you will not bump into in festival week or any other week is the Hay Poisoner, Herbert Armstrong. A solicitor in the town, he was hanged on 31 May 1922 for poisoning his wife

with arsenic. There is, of course, a book about him: *The Hay Poisoner: Herbert Rowse Armstrong* by Martin Beales. But Chatwin also borrowed his character for a minor role in *On the Black Hill*.

Chatwin died in 1989. He had been a very keen walker, some might say fanatical. He believed that walking was a 'sacramental' activity; that by just walking one could make the world a better place:

> 'Next morning, after foddering, he took a stick and walked the nine miles to Bryn Draenog Hill. On reaching the line of rocks that crown the summit, he sat down out of the wind and retied a bootlace. Overhead, puffy clouds were streaming out of Wales, their shadows plunging down the slopes of gorse and heather, slowing up as they moved across the fields of winter wheat.
>
> . . . To the east was the River Wye, a silver ribbon snaking through water-meadows and the whole countryside dotted with white or red-brick farmhouses.'
>
> *On the Black Hill*, Chapter III

Leaving Hay we cross the road bridge over the Wye, which in summer is clear and shallow here, with islands of shingle and shrubs midstream. But like most of the border rivers it is volatile; and in winter after heavy rain it can present a very different aspect: deep, turbulent and loaded with ruddy sediment washed down from the fields and mountains upstream.

Northwards from Hay our route takes us alongside the Wye, before we cross the main Hereford-Brecon road at Bronydd, and enter Bettws Dingle. Here we start to climb into the hills of the old county of Radnorshire, since 1974 part of Powys. Damp and shady in summer, Bettws Dingle may offer a pleasant, cool respite from the hot sun. But it is also notorious for its very vigorous brambles. If these have not been recently cut back you may feel it would be better named Bettws Jungle.

A quieter corner of Hay

River Wye from Hay bridge

Peter Mayes, signkeeper

Honeysuckle, Radnorshire hedgerow

Between the villages of Newchurch and Gladestry the path climbs Disgwylfa Hill which I first walked in March 1987. I was preparing my application for the job of Offa's Dyke Path Officer, and had decided to do some practical research. It was a memorable introduction. The ground was covered with crisp snow, the sky was blue and the sun was shining. The views were stunning and, of course, I took lots of photographs. More recently I walked the hill in summer. This time I had soft turf underfoot and skylarks singing overhead. I have never heard so many skylarks in one place.

Disgwylfa, by the way, is Welsh for 'watching-place', perhaps another sign of the troubled past of this area. There is at least one other Disgwylfa Hill, in South Shropshire, and a couple of miles further north is a Squilver farm, surely an anglicised version of the same word.

At Gladestry – a handy village for walkers because it has both a shop and a pub – lives Peter Mayes. I first met Peter and his wife Margery when I was tutoring an evening class on Offa's Dyke in Kington. Peter subsequently became treasurer of the Offa's Dyke Association, a leading light in the management of the Offa's Dyke Centre, and a very useful volunteer, helping out with odd jobs on the National Trail. A retired army officer, he came here from Berkshire, drawn, at least in part, by the lure of the Offa's Dyke Path.

Peter had a friend who lived in Hawes, in Wensleydale. When Peter visited he was much impressed to find that his friend had a Pennine Way signpost by his gate. 'I want one of those!' he thought. Not long after that, Peter was looking at properties in the Marches and came across a house in Gladestry with an Offa's Dyke Path sign close by the end of the drive. So his mind was made up; only Margery remained to be convinced.

ON
NATURE'S
TRAIL

Hawthorn

The hawthorn (*Crataegus monogyna),* also known as quickthorn, is a shrub intimately involved in man's shaping of the landscape, particularly in England. In the seventeenth and eighteenth centuries the Parliamentary Enclosure Acts divided up huge areas of the countryside into the pattern of fields which we know today. In the lowlands the boundaries between these fields were marked out with newly-planted hedges of the quick-growing hawthorn. This was before the days of barbed wire, but the prickly and robust hawthorn did an effective job of keeping both people and livestock at bay.

To keep hawthorn hedges stock-proof they have to be maintained, by the traditional craft of hedge-laying, which is still very much alive in the Marches. In winter the hedge is thinned and the stems of the stouter shrubs are cut with a billhook just enough to enable them to be bent over and woven into the hedge. During the next season the recumbent stem throws up fresh shoots which grow up through the old hedge to make a densely-woven living barrier to livestock.

Hawthorn is pretty as well as functional. It gives us the sweet-smelling May blossom in spring and the bright red haws (berries) in autumn. And, of course, it tells us when to discard our winter woollies: 'Ne'r cast a clout til (the) May is out'.

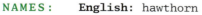

Winter hedge-laying by the Offa's Dyke Path at Gladestry

NAMES: **English:** hawthorn **Latin:** *Crataegus monogyna* **Welsh:** draenen wen (lit. white thorn)

YELLOW RATTLE

The yellow rattle (*Rhinanthus minor*) is another plant whose fortunes are, like those of the hawthorn, intimately connected with changing agricultural practices. Yellow rattle (also known as hay rattle) grows in hay meadows. Its name comes from the flower, which is yellow, and the seed, which rattles inside its pod. The flower appears from May to June and, depending on the weather, grows to seed in late June or early July. By tradition the hay is ready to be mown when the yellow rattle starts to rattle. On the other hand, if the hay is cut earlier than this the plant cannot set seed, and so dies out. This applies to many of the other wild flowers of hay meadows. Since the 1980s, government agricultural grants have become gradually more conservation oriented, and one benefit of this is that farmers are now paid to protect wild flowers by cutting their hay later in the season.

A meadow brown butterfly in a hay meadow

RED KITE

The red kite is a conservation success story. When I came to mid-Wales in the 1980s this majestic bird was a rare sight, largely confined to the Cambrian mountains. In the 1950s the situation had been even worse; my 1959 *Collins Pocket Guide to British Birds*, describes it as 'Resident, breeding only in central Wales, where fewer than a dozen pairs survive, a rare vagrant elsewhere.'

More recently the kite has been gradually expanding its range so that you now have quite a good chance of seeing at least one as you walk the Offa's Dyke Path. Until you get your eye in, it is easy to confuse the kite with the much commoner buzzard. The kite is actually about half as big again as the buzzard, and to my eye has a slightly less elegant flight, but its one unmistakeable feature is its forked tail. It has also been reintroduced to the south-east of England, with startling success, and is now quite a common sight in the relatively tame landscape of the Chiltern Hills. To my considerable surprise I even saw one recently over the M4 near Slough.

NAMES: **English:** yellow rattle   **Latin:** *Rhinanthus minor*   **Welsh:** cribell felen
             English: red kite   **Latin:** *Milvus milvus*   **Welsh:** barcud coch

From Gladestry we climb again, this time onto **Hergest Ridge**. If you are of my generation the name may have a familiar ring. It was the title used in 1974 by musician Mike Oldfield for his second album. His first had been the iconic 'Tubular Bells', the first release of Richard Branson's Virgin Records. Oldfield knew Hergest Ridge well, having lived just the other side of Kington, on Bradnor Hill, close by the Offa's Dyke Path.

Long before the 1970s the name Hergest was made famous in Wales by the Red Book of Hergest (see Digging into History, overleaf).

Another fan of Hergest Ridge is author Sam Llewellyn. Sam has several novels and children's books to his name, including the 'Little Darlings' series published by Puffin. He also writes for the national press, and for our local arts magazine, *Broad Sheep*. I walked up onto the ridge one hot July morning and met Sam coming the other way talking into a mobile phone. Having no idea who he was, and in the absence of any other model, I waited until he had finished and then asked if I could include him in a photograph. Sam told me that he walks the ridge every day, and regards it as his office, so it was very fitting. And there was me thinking that *I* had a nice office.

On Hergest Ridge you will also have the opportunity to review an interesting selection of National Trail waymarks of various periods. There are old concrete fence-posts, once painted white with black acorns. There are shorter cast-concrete signs, of the type known among the cognoscenti as 'tombstones'; and there are more recent and more tasteful oak posts with carved and painted waymarks. Somehow those tombstones seem to conjure up the spirit of the 1960s, which I suspect is when they were first designed. Peter Mayes actually likes them, but then he is an engineer.

Sam Llewellyn in his office

Waymarks on Hergest Ridge

DIGGING INTO HISTORY

Red Book of Hergest

One of the most important Welsh manuscripts from the Middle Ages is actually named after a mansion on the English side of Offa's Dyke, in Herefordshire, where it was kept for many years by the Vaughan family who lived there. The Vaughans of Hergest were well-known for their patronage to poets during the fifteenth and early sixteenth centuries, so it is no surprise that this manuscript which was so carefully preserved over the centuries contains a wide range of poetry. The Red Book of Hergest also includes history, *Brut y Tywysogion*; traditional legends which make up the Mabinogion; a collection of proverbs; the writings of the Physicians of Myddfai, and a Welsh grammar. Remarkably, most of the manuscript is in one hand: it is believed to be the work of one Hywel Fychan, son of Hywel Goch. This, of course, is the 'coch' which gives the work its title – Llyfr Coch Hergest, the Red Book of Hergest. It is kept in the Bodleian Library, Oxford.

Hergest Court

timewatch

2500 BC

The Discoed yew must have started to grow from a mere seedling. Over four millennia later, the ancient yew still graces the churchyard. It defies explanation that of the 200 largest old yews in England and Wales, 79 are in Wales. Powys alone has 43, and there are a further 20 in the border counties of Herefordshire and Shropshire.

1701

The manuscript known as the Red Book of Hergest was given to Jesus College, Oxford, for safe keeping.

1932

Clun Museum was opened, the main exhibit being a display of over 1,000 flints, all collected in and around the Clun Valley. The flints were all prehistoric tools, mostly dating from the Bronze Age and thought to be at least 4000 years old. There were awls, saws, axes and knives, and scrapers of all shapes and sizes.

1988

The Hay Festival was started by Peter Florence, a young actor whose family came from the Black Mountains. The enormously successful literary festival has had a host of famous guests over the years, including Bill Clinton, Norman Mailer, Seamus Heaney and Jo Brand. Apparently Florence funded the first festival with the winnings from a game of poker.

1999

Ian Bapty took up his post as full-time archaeologist on Offa's Dyke and started an intensive programme of conservation.

Conserving Offa's Dyke

Writing in 1926, Sir Cyril Fox lamented the complete disappearance of sections of the dyke which had been surveyed in the 1850s. 'Destruction has been going on more or less continuously,' he reported then.

Most of Offa's Dyke is now protected by law, but sadly it is still being whittled away. Fox would be alarmed to see some sections of the dyke today.

Walkers love Offa's Dyke, but sometimes you can love something too much, and there is no doubt that walkers do damage this ancient earthwork, especially under trees. Closely-cropped turf is the best protective surface but turf grows poorly, if at all, under trees. Shade also stops the ground drying as quickly, and falling leaves add to these effects, often forming a thick, damp mulch. In this situation the tramp of walkers' boots is more likely to do damage. Other 'hot spots' for erosion can occur where walkers have to scramble up or down the sides of the dyke. Their feet exert more pressure here and any disturbed soil will inevitably work its way down the slope. Each time this happens a little bit of dyke is lost.

But walkers are not the only problem. Farmers under pressure to make the most of their land will plough as close as they can to the earthwork, often nicking into the base of the bank. Badgers and rabbits burrow into it; sheep scrape away at its sides to find shelter from the wind. Roads and driveways crossing the dyke are widened. Wind and rain wear away at the bank, while debris fills the ditch. Winter gales batter ageing trees growing on the dyke, and from time to time one gives way, its roots tearing out a chunk of the earthwork as it falls.

But it is not all bad news. From 1999 to 2006, Offa's Dyke had its first full-time archaeologist to address these problems. Ian Bapty carried out practical conservation work and repairs on the earthwork, commented on planning applications which affected the dyke, and met and advised landowners. He arranged tree surgery to prolong the life of trees on the dyke and to let light and air through to the ground below. He cleared scrub to discourage burrowing rabbits and he helped to install timber staircases, which enable walkers to get safely up and down the slope of the dyke without damaging the surface.

Staircase at Evanjobb

Sheep grazing the earthwork

From Hergest Ridge the National Trail descends into Kington, via Ridgebourne Road. A nice touch which you will find as you approach the town, whether from north or south, is a 'Welcome to Kington' sign specifically placed for the benefit of Offa's Dyke Path users. Kington is (just) in Herefordshire and therefore England, but is often confused with Knighton, which is (just) in Powys and therefore Wales. As well as having similar names and being on the border, both towns have the Offa's Dyke Path passing through them, so the confusion is not surprising.

Kington is a staging-post on the National Trail and, since there is no other substantial settlement between here and Knighton, you would be well-advised to stock up with provisions for the day before you move on.

After Kington it is uphill again, to Bradnor Hill and then Rushock Hill. On the latter, you will rejoin the dyke itself, the first time you'll set foot on it since Monmouth. There are occasional sections of the earthwork dotted about Herefordshire, but between here and Llangollen you will rarely be far from it.

Crossing the valley of the Hindwell Brook, you leave Herefordshire for the last time. The next valley is that of the Lugg, where a short detour can be taken to Discoed and the lovely little church of St Michael, with its famous yew tree. The yew is very, very old, but yew is notoriously difficult to date. Richard Mabey, in his *Flora Britannica*, reports that by one method of calculation the Discoed yew could be as much as 4,500 years old. But he stresses that this is extremely difficult to verify.

Most of the Friends of St Michael's Discoed are a good deal younger than this, but they are a pretty impressive bunch nonetheless, especially when it comes to fundraising. They have filled the much larger St Andrew's Church at Presteigne for concerts of baroque music, and on one occasion they persuaded me and my colleague Ian Bapty to lead a guided walk along the dyke for them.

There are other very old trees around Discoed, notably stately oaks growing atop Offa's Dyke.

A welcome sign for walkers

Oaks on Offa's Dyke

But you have probably already worked out that if they grow on the dyke they can only be a fraction of the age of the St Michael's yew.

Just past Discoed we cross the river Lugg. Look out for dippers and kingfishers. Both birds fly fast and low along streams and rivers, so that by the time you realise what they are, they will probably have disappeared. There are otters on this river too, but you would be very lucky indeed if you see one. The bridge over the Lugg is called Dolley Old Bridge, and the hamlet just beyond is Dolley Green. They are pretty and memorable names, probably a corruption of the Welsh 'dolau', meaning 'meadows'.

One more climb before Knighton, this time onto Furrow Hill, from which a continuous ridge walk takes us over Hawthorn Hill and Hengwm Hill to Rhos-y-meirch. At Rhos-y-meirch there is a short but unavoidable section of road walking, which briefly takes us away from the line of the earthwork.

Once we leave the road at Rhos-y-meirch we follow the line of the dyke until we descend into Knighton. In this short section there is great variation in the state of the earthwork. At first the dyke is clear, its presence emphasised by a belt of larch trees, but soon the path follows it across a field where there is nothing left to see but a barely perceptible rise in the ground. Further on there is a very well-preserved section, fenced off from the fields and covered in broadleaved trees, then the path crosses to the other side of the dyke which suddenly becomes nothing more than a hedgebank, indistinguishable from the boundaries of the surrounding fields.

This section makes a very useful bite-sized introduction to the Offa's Dyke Path in all its variety. And in the town of Knighton at its end, there are plenty of resting-places and sources of refreshment for the weary.

River Lugg at Dolley bridge

On Hawthorn Hill

Chapter V : Clun Forest

Now we reach my favourite part of the Offa's Dyke Path: the South Shropshire Hills. Quiet, remote and picturesque, the hills often catch out those walkers who have not studied their contour lines. Don't be too ambitious in estimating the miles you will cover in your first day out from Knighton.

But first, enjoy the town where I have lived for the past nineteen years.

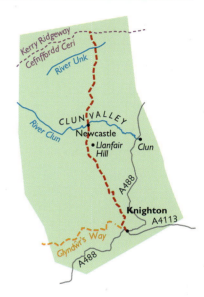

My first impression of **Knighton** – when I came to stay at the Youth Hostel in 1987 – was of a quiet, small, country town nestling among hills, set against the green backdrop of Kinsley Wood. The wood takes up the whole of the northern side of the valley here: town and wood face each other across the river Teme, so nearly every part of the town has a view of trees. I had that view from my office at the Offa's Dyke Centre and from season to season, I never tired of it.

One of the town's key landmarks has to be the clock tower at the top of Broad Street. Many of the towns of mid-Wales and the border have a clock tower as a focal point, and Knighton's, built in 1872, is virtually identical to that in Hay-on-Wye, built in 1881. In *The Buildings of Wales: Powys*, Richard Haslam describes Hay's tower as 'off-the-peg Gothic'. I have often wondered how you would go about buying an off-the-peg clock tower. Presumably not off a peg. Was there a catalogue, as there was for such things as decorative plasterwork and fireplaces? Did the good burghers of Hay realise that theirs was a second-hand design? Or was there a cunning architect involved, who calculated that no one from Hay would ever have reason to go to Knighton, and so pocketed two fees for one job? And anyway, is Knighton's the original or is there another elsewhere?

As the Welsh have long since recognized, the most prestigious landmark of Trefyclo or Trefyclawdd – dyke's town – is Offa's Dyke itself. It is the only town actually built on the dyke, which still runs right through it. According to 1930s archaeologist Sir Cyril Fox, the town was originally built in a triangular defensive enclosure which had Offa's Dyke along one side, the river Teme on another and the valley or cwm of the Wylcwm Brook on the third. It is difficult to imagine this now that the dyke is surrounded by twentieth-century houses, and The Cwm is a picturesque backwater full of cottages and gardens.

Thursday is market day in Knighton. The livestock market is run by McCartneys, a local firm which has operated in the area since 1874. Traditionally this is the day when the farmers and other country people come down from the surrounding hills to do all their town business: buy and sell

Clock tower, Broad Street

Livestock market, Knighton

livestock, shop, visit the bank and the doctor, maybe get a haircut and, if they have had a profitable morning, visit the pub. Lambs, cull ewes and cull cows are sold at the auction yard every Thursday, and there's another livestock market on alternate Fridays for store lambs and store cattle.

Knighton is a friendly and unpretentious town and was just the kind of place I had always wanted to live. And managing the Offa's Dyke Path was just the kind of job I had always wanted to do; so much so that I had applied for it twice. The first time was in 1982, when I was unsuccessful. So I went off and got some more experience before applying again in 1987 – and when I got the job, I stuck to it for 18 years!

Another Englishman who, like me, strayed into Knighton and found himself staying, is Andy Hazell. He is, without doubt, a creative man. You name it, he'll make it for you. And if you already have one, he'll film it. He describes himself as 'a maker of things, large and small'. When pressed to elaborate, he says that he is also a public artist, craftsperson and stop-frame animated film-maker. While I was talking to him in his kitchen, an arts centre in Scunthorpe rang, asking him to run a workshop on making tinplate automata. Outside the back door stood a freshly-painted model of the Eiffel tower, about 6 foot tall. He had made this to put in the garden for sweet peas to climb.

Andy was born in Altrincham, studied Art at the University of Reading, and lived for several years in Hull. One fateful day, on his way to Presteigne to buy a harmonium, he went slightly astray and spotted the old Victorian primary school in Knighton which was displaying a 'For Sale' sign. At that time the Offa's Dyke Centre was housed in the school, so he scrounged a piece of paper from Rebe Brick, Centre Manager, and put in a bid there and then. Somewhat to his surprise the bid was successful and the school has since become his home, workshop and store. Now, he complains, all his work has to be designed to fit through the 41-inch side door of the building.

Andy's outdoor sculptures and huge models can be seen in Cardiff and Swansea and east of Offa's Dyke in Leeds, Burton on Trent, Bradford and Canterbury. When I visited him a couple of

Early morning, Knighton livestock market

Andy Hazell and his lair

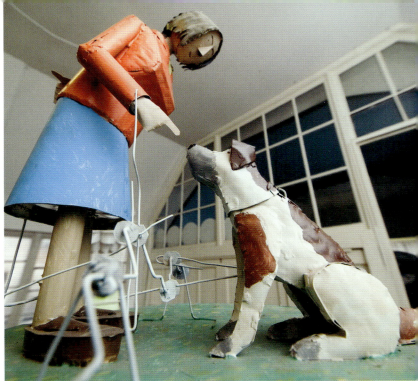

years ago he was making a clockwork model of the solar system which I next saw in the foyer of Broadcasting House in Cardiff. Not long after that I recognised it on television, in an episode of *Dr Who*.

The little tinplate people which spring to life when a handle is turned are quirky and memorable. One is a lady hoovering, another is a man twisting a little finger in his ear (you need to see it really). And if more variety were needed, *HMS Axminster* is a ship made from an old carpet. You see what I mean about 'creative'.

The Offa's Dyke Path takes you up Broad Street, Knighton's main shopping street, and at the clock tower another National Trail branches off, heading out west into mid-Wales. This is Glyndŵr's Way, which meanders across the remote hills of Radnorshire and Montgomeryshire to Llanidloes and Machynlleth, before returning eastward to Welshpool, where a link back to the Offa's Dyke Path can be made.

If you are walking the Offa's Dyke Path you will almost certainly know of the Offa's Dyke Centre. It is *the* place for information about the National Trail. Here the Offa's Dyke Association runs an official Tourist Information Centre, exhibition and shop. Whether you make your purchases in person, by mail-order or on the internet, you can get maps of the whole route, a range of guidebooks, accommodation and camping lists, and a variety of other useful publications, not to mention T-shirts and assorted other souvenirs: all from very cheerful and helpful staff. The centre provides similar services for Glyndŵr's Way too. Truly a one-stop shop. But that's not all – you can even get married here!

The Offa's Dyke Path goes right by the door of the Offa's Dyke Centre, and then sets off across the park and down through the grassy amphitheatre of Pinner's Hole to the river Teme. After following the river upstream for about 500 yards or so, the path crosses to the other bank by a footbridge. A pedestrian level-crossing then takes it over the Heart of Wales raiway by Panpunton Farm. With a bit of planning, you might catch a nostalgic steam excursion on this line.

Arriving at the Offa's Dyke Centre

'The Lancashire Fusilier' approaching Panpunton Farm

MOUNTAIN PANSY

The cheerful little Mountain Pansy nods in the breeze on the flank of the dyke on Llanfair Hill. Richard Mabey's *Flora Brittanica* reports that the Mountain Pansy was abundant in Shropshire as recently as the 1940s, but has since declined.

It is a member of the violet family, but varies greatly in colour, from violet to yellow, with various mixtures in between.

NAMES:
English: Mountain pansy
Latin: *Viola lutea*
Welsh: Trilliw y mynydd

Wildlife in Knighton

With wildlife in abundance in the countryside on each side, why look for it in the town? Well, small country towns do have their particular flora and fauna. If you find yourself in Knighton on a summer's evening it is difficult not to notice the flocks of swifts which gather over the town and race screaming around the rooftops. Swift is the perfect name for them: they are built for speed, with slender bodies and narrow scythe-shaped wings, raked back like fighter-planes. They spend most of their lives in the air, feeding on flying insects. You may spot a swift swooping up under the eaves and then disappearing – they like to get through a gap and into the roof-space of an old building to build their nests. And of course when such buildings are modernised or re-roofed, the swifts lose their nesting-site. Architects and builders please note.

The jackdaw is a less stylish bird than the swift, but nevertheless is one of the more attractive members of the crow family, with its dandy grey bonnet, particularly bright in spring. Jackdaws too seem to like old buildings. In Knighton they often gather on the roof and tower of the church, but you are also very likely to hear their raucous, clattering 'chicker-chack, chicker chack' calls around the castles and ruined abbeys on either side of the Offa's Dyke Path.

Knighton has a wealth of crumbling stone walls built with lime mortar, an ideal growing medium for the red (and white, and pink) valerian. The valerian's natural habitat is cliffs and rocky outcrops, and it has an amazing ability to grow in next to no soil, even in a stack of old quarry tiles. Its nectar-rich florets are very attractive to moths and butterflies.

The vibrant hues of valerian can be seen in abundance in amongst the buildings of Knighton

The humming bird hawkmoth inserts its proboscis into one floret at a time to feed. Its wings move so fast that even an electronic flash does not completely freeze their motion.

The tower of St Edward's Church, Knighton on a summer's evening, home to swift (above) and jackdaw (below).

NAMES: **English:** jackdaw
Latin: *Corvus monedula*
Welsh: jac-y-do

English: swift
Latin: *Apus apus*
Welsh: gwennol ddu

English: red valerian
Latin: *Centranthus ruber*
Welsh: triaglog goch

The next part of the route is not so easy. **Panpunton Hill** is a stiff climb, and can also be quite slippery when wet. This is a foretaste of things to come. The Knighton to Montgomery section of the National Trail is nicknamed 'the Switchback', and for good reason. Both the dyke and the path cross the grain of the landscape here, going from south to north, across ridges and valleys which all run from west to east. There are four more stiff climbs like this in the next 17 miles, with some only slightly less testing ones in between. But once you crest Panpunton Hill there's a pleasant ridge walk along the dyke to Cwm-sanaham Hill. The river Teme meanders very prettily below, and on a clear day you can see southwards as far back as the Black Mountains.

The trig point on Cwm-sanaham Hill has even more impressive views: a complete 360° panorama. From the stile here look north-west along the dyke and see how it lines up perfectly with the tree-covered section above Garbett Hall.

Now the path dips down again past the solitary cottage at Brynorgan. This was the scene of the Yuletide badger monitoring to which I referred in the first chapter. Eventually you'll reach the cool and leafy dingle near **Garbett Hall**, where a footbridge crosses a little brook. On the bridge, wood sorrel (*Oxalis acetosella*) grows, and among the trees are marsh-marigolds (*Caltha palustris*).

Once through the farmyard at Garbett Hall the path goes uphill once again, on a deeply-rutted farm track alongside the dyke. Note the evidence of extensive badger activity here on the earthwork itself.

On **Llanfair Hill** you are once more on top of the world. A glorious place to be on a clear summer's day, with views in all directions. I was up here in July with a crew from ARD TV of Germany. They had travelled up from London the same day, and the producer was very taken with the tranquillity of Llanfair Hill. As he looked across to Shropshire's Long Mynd, he said, 'I cannot hear a car, and I cannot see any human habitation.' What we could hear was sheep, grasshoppers and the occasional skylark. And yes, there was a low-flying military helicopter; but that was soon gone.

Wood sorrel

View from Llanfair Hill

Castles for warring peoples

The castle that still stands in Montgomery today was constructed by command of Henry III and granted to Hubert de Burgh in 1224. During the Wars of Welsh Independence, it was an important military base for the English forces – this after Llywelyn ap Gruffydd had taken it in 1265 – that Last Welsh Prince again!

CENTRE: *Clun Castle, northeast of Knighton, was built by the Fitzalan family, lords of Clun, in 1195. The dyke did not stop it being attacked at least twice by Welsh Princes: Llywelyn ap Iorwerth, in the thirteenth century, and Owain Glyndŵr, in the fifteenth.*

In border country there is, as one might expect, an abundance of castles and defences. Just in the town of Knighton itself, there are two castles The first, a motte-and-bailey whose shape can still be identified despite the vegetation of the centuries, would seem to have been built about 1100. The second, unusually, is in the back garden of a private house, on Castle Bank. Built by William de Braose around 1200, it fell to Llywelyn ap Gruffydd, Prince of Wales, in 1262. Llywelyn, now remembered as the Last Prince of Wales, was not only a successful warrior but a shrewd and determined politician. King Henry III of England acknowledged Llywelyn's title of Prince of Wales, but when Henry's son, Edward I, came to the throne, it was a different story. Llywelyn refused to pay homage to an English monarch and in return Edward declared war on Wales in 1277. A savage series of battles ensued – and Llywelyn himself was killed in 1282.

785

Offa, powerful king of Mercia, commissions the building of the dyke. It consists of rampart and ditch (on the Welsh side), forming a drop of roughly 26 feet and offers highly advantageous viewing points.

1223

Construction begins on a grand castle at Montgomery – which just has to be called New Montgomery because a motte-and-bailey, known as Hen Domen, has existed there since the eleventh century.

1282

On December 11th, Llywelyn ap Gruffydd is killed at Cilmeri, near Builth. This day is still commemorated by Welsh patriots in the twenty-first century.

1858

The Knighton Railway Company is formed by local landowners and businessmen and work begins on a line between Craven Arms and Knighton. Workmen come from far afield to build the railway and four extra policemen are taken on to deal with the increase in

1872

Knighton's clock tower is built and a virtually identical one is erected in Hay-on-Wye in 1881

1999

The Offa's Dyke Association opens a new purpose-built building in Knighton, the Offa's Dyke Centre

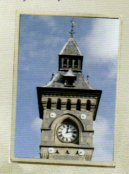

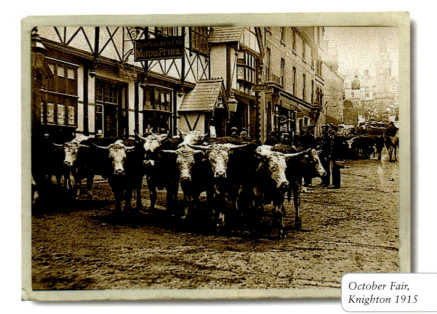

October Fair, Knighton 1915

KNIGHTON – A MARKET TOWN

Borderlands may be famous for fortifications and disputes but, more productively, they are also important areas for trade. Nowhere is this better exemplified than in the long history of sheep fairs and cattle markets at Knighton. The Welsh uplands – too harsh an environment for much arable farming – have traditionally been used for rearing livestock, particularly sheep, and in the border market towns hardy Welsh lambs are sold on for fattening in the English lowlands. On fair days – and there were many of them – Knighton would have been transformed. With cattle and horses loose on the main street and traders in holiday spirit, it obviously drew the children out of school. Many schools gave up the struggle and just closed.

Knighton National Boys School, 2nd October, 1884:
'A Holiday. Fair. Road blocked up with Cattle.'

Of course, concerns about poor attendance is a very common theme in school logbooks of the Victorian era, and the agricultural year certainly affected a town such as Knighton. It would be a long time before rural families accepted that schooling was as important as real life.

Although you are surrounded by green fields you are 1,400 ft (430 m) high here 850 feet higher than the valley floor at Knighton. That July day we had hot sun beating down on us, but in winter there is often a cutting wind. In either case there is very little shelter. Sheep often seek shade under the only available tree, a rather stunted rowan, which has featured in many of my photographs.

Llanfair Hill, and the adjacent Spring Hill, offer one of the most impressive and most easily accessible sections of Offa's Dyke. An uninterrupted sweep of earthwork curves across both hills. The Spring Hill section is easily visible from the minor road which leads down to Cwm Collo from the crossroads by Springhill Farm. Heading south from this road a rough stone byway carries the National Trail up to the dyke on Llanfair Hill. Running alongside the earthwork, first on one side and then the other, this track offers relatively easy walking, with excellent views both of dyke and landscape. If you're not a keen walker, though, a handy leaflet giving directions to Llanfair Hill by road is available at the Offa's Dyke Centre in Knighton.

At Springhill Farm Mr and Mrs Evans provide bed and breakfast, camping and teas for passing walkers. I took the ARD TV crew there to recover from the heat after our expedition to Llanfair Hill. We sat and drank tea in the shade of some beech trees beside the farmhouse. Also enjoying the shade were two visiting Canadians, who were being entertained by the Evans's latest puppy. The puppy will probably be grown up by the time you get there, but Bobby the three-legged farm dog may well still be about. Bobby had cancer, and Mr Evans was faced with the choice of having him put down or spending £400 on an operation which would leave him with a three-legged dog. He chose the operation. Who says farmers are not sentimental?

From Springhill Farm the path and dyke descend side by side into the Clun valley, passing a cottage somewhat confusingly called 'Scotland', where Tara Paul lives, right next to yet another badger sett. A Punjabi who was born in Uganda, Tara has lived at Scotland for 20 years.

Bobby at Springhill Farm

Feeling the heat on Llanfair Hill

She rather liked the badgers – until they broke into her garden, and dug up and ate all her tulip bulbs. Apparently they are quite partial to her gooseberries too, and are absolutely no respecters of persons.

Climbing the path just above Scotland I met Dutch walkers Willem and Hilde Bogtstra from Friesland. They were spending eleven days on the Offa's Dyke Path, walking from Llandegla to Chepstow. The path had been recommended to them as 'beautiful' and they said they had not been disappointed.

Now we are on my favourite part of the Offa's Dyke Path, deep in the South Shropshire Hills, celebrated by A.E. Houseman in his collection of poems *A Shropshire Lad*. The poems were first published in 1896, but many of his descriptions are remarkably apt to this day. You really get the feeling that not a lot has changed here in the last hundred years.

Clunton and Clunbury,　　　　　*In valleys of springs of rivers,*
Clungunford and Clun,　　　　　*By Ony and Teme and Clun,*
Are the quietest places　　　　　*The country for easy livers,*
under the sun.　　　　　　　　*The quietest under the sun.*

I am sure the local farmers would dispute the bit about 'easy livers', but these villages are still some of the quietest places, at least under the sun we see in this country.

A hearty day's walking can be enjoyed by crossing the river Clun, going over the switchback into more forgotten valleys, over the tiny river Unk and through the charmingly-named Nut Wood, before finally crossing back into Wales at the ancient Kerry Ridgeway.

Willem and Hilde Bogtstra

Offa's Dyke and the Clun valley at Maytime

Chapter VI : The Severn Valley

The next part of our journey rarely takes us far from the Wales-England border. We start by crossing into Wales at the ancient Kerry Ridgeway, but soon return to Shropshire at Brompton Bridge. Thereafter we cross back and forth as we follow a section of Offa's Dyke which still marks the border today. Eventually we come to Llanymynech, where one side of the main street is in Wales, and the other in England.

We are in relatively low-lying country here, alongside both the river Severn and the Montgomery Canal. So there is plenty of aquatic wildlife, but also no shortage of history or industrial archaeology.

At the **Kerry Ridgeway** we are on the Wales-England border again, on a country lane which looks much like any other in South Shropshire. But this country lane is widely believed to be at least twice as old as Offa's Dyke. Its exact prehistoric origins may be debatable but the ridgeway was almost certainly also used as a drove road in the seventeenth and eighteenth centuries. Shirley Toulson, in her book *The Drovers Roads of Wales*, thought so, and the Clwyd-Powys Archaeological Trust (CPAT) cites the road's wide verges in support of this idea. It may well have been in use in medieval times too – the earthwork-castle of Bishop's Moat, close by the ridgeway two miles east of Offa's Dyke, is possible evidence of this.

Northwards from the Kerry Ridgeway we descend with the dyke to emerge on another narrow lane, close by the entrance to Drewyn farm, where Ceinwen Richards provides both teas and bed and breakfast. Ceinwen's sign was a very welcome sight when I arrived here one summer's evening about ten years ago, having walked 'the Switchback' from Newcastle on Clun with a group of colleagues. Large quantities of tea and cake were consumed, accompanied by sighs of contentment.

If you prefer something stronger than tea you may like to press on along the dyke through the grounds of Mellington Hall – now a hotel with plenty of Gothic atmosphere and serving a good dinner – to the **Blue Bell** at Brompton crossroads. The Blue Bell is a traditional landmark on the Offa's Dyke Path, built on top of the dyke itself, with the National Trail passing by its door. As you go by, note the humped profile of the car park on the south side of the inn. That's Offa's Dyke under there. The inn is a welcome refreshment stop for walkers, a quiet unpretentious little country pub which you could easily pass without noticing, and the first one since leaving Newcastle on Clun. It has been in the hands of the Jones family since 1926. The Blue Bell has also been popular with archaeologists for many years. Teams from Manchester University's extra-mural department, under the charismatic leadership of Dr David Hill, used the Blue Bell as a base for their regular summer excavations along Offa's Dyke.

The Blue Bell at Brompton crossroads

The dyke by the Kerry Ridgeway

To see **Montgomery** you need to take a little detour to the west from the Offa's Dyke Path. It is well worth a visit, though, so if your itinerary does not allow it, come back another time. There is an excellent ruined castle (the third in the town's history) and lots of beautiful red-brick Georgian buildings. If the town's English name sounds a little French, that is because it is. It is named after the Norman earl, Roger de Montgomery, and was county town of Montgomeryshire until 1974, despite being smaller than many villages.

According to the 1969 *Shell Guide to Wales*, no new buildings were erected in Montgomery between 1799 and 1939. Yes, 140 years without any builders! Imagine that. But even after 1939 the place did not exactly take off. Richard Haslam in *The Buildings of Wales: Powys* praises its calm: 'With its hilly site and views over Shropshire to Corndon Hill, Montgomery is a delightful place, and as quiet as could be.'

Like the Blue Bell, **Little Brompton** is something of an institution on the Offa's Dyke Path. For as long as anyone can remember Bob and Gaynor Bright have been providing bed and breakfast and camping for National Trail walkers. I stayed at Little Brompton back in 1993, when filming for BBC 2's *Travel Show*. On that occasion, presenter Carol Smillie stayed up the hill with Ceinwen Richards at Drewyn.

Both path and dyke cross the farm and Mr Bright is more than happy to have them; he has successfully blended the National Trail into his farm business, which for the most part has been to the advantage of all. In 2001 it all went horribly wrong though, when foot-and-mouth disease struck the UK, and for a while the whole of the Rights of Way network, including the Offa's Dyke Path, was closed.

Mid-Wales was one of the areas worst affected by foot-and-mouth disease, and Welshpool market was identified as a centre from which the disease had spread. On 21 March 2001, a date indelibly stamped on Gaynor Bright's memory, stock at Little Brompton was found to be infected.

Georgian Montgomery

Cattle graze Offa's Dyke near Montgomery

Nightmare of 2001

Happier times at Little Brompton

All of the Bright's animals then had to be destroyed and their farm was quarantined, which meant that for the better part of the peak summer months they had no income from visitors either. It is a year they will never forget.

Northwards from Little Brompton for about 2 miles (3 km) is one of those sections of Offa's Dyke which still mark the border between Wales and England. The National Trail actually runs alongside the earthwork here, crossing occasionally from the Welsh side to the English, but Offa's Dyke itself is split right down the middle, the eastern flank being under the watchful eye of English Heritage, the western under that of its Welsh equivalent, Cadw.

After passing through the straggling hamlet of Forden, and then Kingswood, our path starts to climb the hill known as the Long Mountain, in a deeply-sunken lane. There is more to this road than meets the eye: glance through one of the gateways on the left and you'll see that the road surface is about level with the fields to the west. The high bank between the two is in fact Offa's Dyke, here on quite a substantial scale. And this time we can confidently say that there was a well-trodden way here some hundreds of years before the dyke was built. For this is the line of a Roman road which led from Forden Gaer ('caer' is the Welsh word for 'a fort'), near Montgomery, over the Long Mountain to the Roman city of Wroxeter, then fourth largest in Britain. Wroxeter is now a small village by the Severn, south-east of Shrewsbury, but it still has substantial Roman remains. After about half a mile, dyke and path turn away from the tarmac surface, but as the Roman road continues along the ridge its verges becomes wider and wider until it seems to meander between distant hedges. Another drovers' route perhaps. It is easy to imagine great herds of cattle slowing down to spread out and graze here on their journey to the English lowlands.

Leighton Woods lie ahead. The Leighton estate was developed in the mid-nineteenth century, and the interiors at Leighton Hall were designed by the famous team of J.G. Crace and A.W.N. Pugin, who decorated the Houses of Parliament. The estate used state-of-the-art technology, having

continued on p. 106

ON NATURE'S TRAIL

Wetland Flowers

Between Buttington Bridge and Llanymynech you will walk beside both the river Severn and the Montgomery Canal so there's plenty of opportunity to enjoy some of the plants which thrive in a watery environment.

The alien invader **himalayan or Indian balsam** (*Impatiens glandulifera*), a relative of the houseplant busy Lizzy, grows along the banks of the Severn and many other British rivers. It is attractive enough, with prominent purple flowers which have a distinctive sickly-sweet perfume, but it is spreading rapidly, aided by very impressive exploding seed pods which burst and shower seeds in every direction when touched. They're a big hit with children of all ages. There is a large colony a few fields north of Buttington Bridge.

Wild Iris (*Iris pseudacorus*), also known as Yellow Flag, is an elegant native very like the garden iris, *Iris germanica*, but with yellow flowers which are slightly smaller and less showy.

NAMES:

English: Himalayan or Indian balsam
Latin: *Impatiens glandulifera*
Welsh: jac y neidiwr

English: wild or yellow iris
Latin: *Iris pseudacorus*
Welsh: gellesgen

MEADOWSWEET

Meadowsweet typically grows in meadows, roadside ditches and other damp places, but also in profusion along the banks of the Montgomery Canal. The clusters of cream flowers have a subtle sweet fragrance. An earlier Latin name for meadowsweet was *Spiraea ulmaria* which, according to Richard Mabey, gives us the word 'aspirin'. Both meadowsweet and willow naturally contain the active ingredient of aspirin: salicylic acid. It has a variety of names in Welsh, including *chwys Arthur* (Arthur's sweat), *llysiau blodau'r mêl* (honey flowers) and, best of all, *brenhines y weirglodd* (queen of the meadows).

NAMES:
English: meadowsweet
Latin: *Filipendula ulmaria*
Welsh: erwain

*NATURE FILE * NATURE FILE * NATURE FILE*

AT HOME ON THE WATER

The whole of the Montgomery Canal is designated a Site of Special Scientific Interest (SSSI) because of its aquatic wildlife. So you won't be surprised to see mallard ducks and (in spring) fluffy ducklings paddling up and down. There are mute swans too; a few years ago one nested by the canal right in the middle of Llanymynech. You will need a quicker eye to spot damselflies and dragonflies, but they are there.

The damselfly pictured here is a (male) banded demoiselle (*Calopteryx splendens*), perched on the banks of the Severn close by the Offa's Dyke Path in late June. Damselflies are similar to dragonflies, but are generally smaller and fold their wings parallel to their body when at rest. Dragonflies hold their wings out straight both in flight and at rest. Both dragonflies and damselflies are found near water, where their larvae develop.

NAMES: **English:** damselfly   **Latin:** *Calopteryx splendens*   **Welsh:** mursen

its own gasworks as well as elaborate water, gas and fertiliser distribution systems. Its chicken house, which really is a rather fine house, but with very small doors, was famous. Modern forestry was pioneered here too, and there is a magnificent plantation of giant redwood trees, managed by the Royal Forestry Society. Sadly the estate as a whole is *not* open to the public.

After Leighton Woods there is one more climb, to **Beacon Ring**, an Iron Age hill-fort, before the descent to the Severn valley. From Beacon Ring there's a grand view across to **Powis Castle**, which, with its magnificent terraced gardens, is deservedly one of the National Trust's most visited properties. I am a regular there myself.

To cross the river Severn the National Trail has to share a bridge with the A458 trunk road, and to be perfectly frank, Buttington Bridge isn't big enough for both of them. It is an elegant, single span cast-iron bridge, and a listed structure, but it was built in 1872, long before the days of the articulated lorry, and there is no footway. So please proceed with extreme caution.

Two parts of our route to Llanymynech follow the **Montgomeryshire Canal** (usually abbreviated to 'Montgomery Canal'). These are between Buttington and Pool Quay, and, later between Four Crosses and Llanymynech. In both cases, walkers are saved a dangerous and unpleasant walk along the main A483 trunk road.

The Montgomery Canal was opened between 1796 and 1819, and linked to the Shropshire Union canal network via the Llangollen Canal at Frankton. It is a 'narrow' canal, designed to carry 70ft long by 6ft wide narrow boats. One of the canal's major functions was to carry limestone from the Llanymynech quarries, and limekilns were also built along the route of the canal.

There is plenty of wildlife along the canal which is officially designated a Site of Special Scientific Interest. It was closed to navigation in 1936 but has been undergoing restoration, a section at a time, for many years and boats can now be hired at Welshpool.

Kitty Thomson, aged four, enjoying Offa's Dyke

Powis Castle

DIGGING INTO HISTORY

Limestone, limekilns and lime

Limekilns at Craignant

One important function of the Montgomery Canal was to distribute limestone quarried at Llanymynech. As well being used for masonry, this limestone was crushed and burned to make lime for the building industry and for agriculture. This was done in specially built limekilns. Coal and limestone were fed in at the top for burning and subsequently the product, quicklime, was raked out at the bottom. When water was added to this a chemical reaction produced slaked lime.

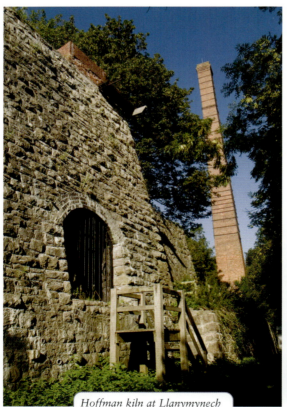
Hoffman kiln at Llanymynech

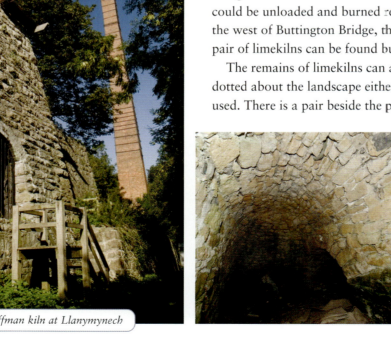

Lime was used in the building industry to make mortar for bricklaying (before the invention of Portland Cement), and plaster for interior and exterior walls. In agriculture it was spread on the land to make the soil less acid.

According to the Clwyd-Powys Archaeological Trust there were 92 limekilns along a 26-mile stretch of the Montgomery Canal in 1840/41, where limestone could be unloaded and burned ready for local use. At Buttington Cross, a little to the west of Buttington Bridge, there is a picnic site on the bank of the canal, where a pair of limekilns can be found buried in the undergrowth

The remains of limekilns can also be seen elsewhere on the Offa's Dyke Path, dotted about the landscape either where limestone was quarried or where lime was used. There is a pair beside the path at Craignant in Shropshire, and another just above the path at Eglwyseg Rocks, north of Llangollen.

The use of lime mortars and plasters in building have enjoyed a revival in recent years. This reflects increased awareness of the conservation of old buildings, and also of the high energy demands of Portland Cement production. Remember the tower at Llangattock Lingoed church?

1109

Cadwgan ap Bleddyn started work on a fortification on the site where Powis Castle stands today. The present building came later, in the thirteenth century, and was home to the earls of Powys over many centuries.

1748

Montgomery Town Hall, one of the lovely Georgian buildings in the town, was built by William Baker, for the Herbert family, for whom he was then working at Powis Castle. The clock tower was not added until 1921.

1796

Part of the Montgomery-shire Canal was opened. Horse-drawn narrow boats carried limestone as well as other agricultural cargoes. Carreghofa Locks, pictured here, were restored to their former glory in 1996.

2001

Foot-and-mouth disease caused devastation to the farming industry throughout much of the UK. In mid-Wales, nearly all stock had to be destroyed and the countryside reeked of burning carcasses.

The Cold War at Criggion

Until 2003 the Severn valley between Pool Quay and Llanymynech was dominated by a network of huge radio masts which formed the Criggion long-wave radio transmitter. This was a top-secret military installation believed to have been used for communication with ships and submarines all around the world during the Cold War. A network of cables was strung from steel masts up to 720 feet (220 m) tall.

Criggion radio station was first built on the east bank of the Severn in 1942, at the height of the Second World War. It was intended as back-up for the main transmitter at Rugby in Warwickshire (visible until recently beside the M1), in case that should be bombed. Later, both Criggion and Rugby are claimed to have been used to maintain contact with the Royal Navy's nuclear submarines. A such they would have been prime targets in the event of nuclear war.

Criggion survived into the twenty-first century, but was finally demolished in August 2003. The Offa's Dyke Path runs along the opposite bank of the river here, just a few hundred yards from the masts, and had to be closed for a short period during the demolition

While walking the Montgomery Canal towpath you may well come across the narrow boat Heulwen-Sunshine. The brainchild of the late Claude Millington, this canal boat was built in the 1970s by apprentices at the Cammel Laird shipyard at Birkenhead to a special design for carrying passengers with a range of disabilities. *Heulwen* is regularly used by groups of disabled people from all over Wales, the Midlands and Merseyside, who enjoy a day trip along the canal.

At Pool Quay we descend to the floodplain of the river Severn, and walk on top of an artificial floodbank known as an *argae* – the Welsh word for 'dam', but a word in everyday use among English-speaking river engineers in this area. At first sight, these floodbanks appear to have been built to keep the river off the surrounding farmland but what they do is actually rather more clever than that. The Severn is a notoriously volatile river. Heavy rain or snow around its upper reaches in the Welsh mountains quickly send a flood surge downstream to English riverside towns such as Shrewsbury, Ironbridge and Tewkesbury. When the river reaches dangerously high levels the argae enables water to be diverted from the main channel onto the surrounding fields, where it can be stored, thereby limiting flood levels downstream. When the threat subsides, the water is released. The flow of water on and off the fields is controlled by sluice gates, one of which we walk across near Derwas Bridge.

No one is quite sure when flood defences were first built on this part of the Severn, but records show that some existed in the eighteenth century when Thomas Telford was surveyor for Shropshire. This would make the argae about the same age as the Montgomery Canal, and there are similarities in the design of bridges used on the canal and the argae, which suggest that the same engineer worked on both.

At Derwas Bridge we leave one argae and, floods permitting, cross a low-lying field to join another. Turn left here and head toward The Nea. (If you turn right you will find yourself on the Severn Way, and heading back, the long way, to Sedbury.) Somewhere along here, no one is quite sure where, this argae merges seamlessly into Offa's Dyke, and we are back to business as usual.

Flood at Derwas

Heulwen-Sunshine

Chapter VII : North Shropshire Hills

The next excursion starts with a climb through limestone quarries rich in both wildlife and industrial archaeology. Through the uplands of north-west Shropshire, Welsh place-names abound. And back in the Ceiriog valley, there can be no doubt that this is the land of song and poetry.

Offa's Dyke is close to the walker's path for most of this journey, though at Chirk Castle it takes a brief dip in an ornamental lake.

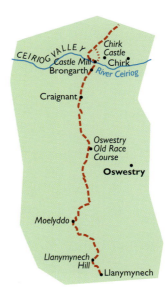

Llanymynech is a fascinating place. *Mynach,* by the way, is the Welsh word for 'monk', and Llanymynech means the village, or church, of the monks. The present church is in fact a Victorian one, dedicated to St Agatha. Though Llanymynech's name is Welsh, half of the village is in England. The border runs along the main street, so that the houses on one side are in Wales, and face across to neighbours who are in England. Archaeologist Sir Cyril Fox, writing in 1928, suggested that this may be because the street follows the original line of Offa's Dyke.

Behind the village rise the rocky cliffs of Llanymynech Hill. Many, if not all, of these cliffs are actually artificial, formed by centuries of quarrying for limestone. Stone from the quarries was winched down to the bottom of the hill on steeply-sloping railway tracks. The engineered gradients on which these tracks were laid were called 'inclined planes', and the same technology was commonly used in the slate quarries of north Wales. At the bottom of the hill, the limestone was loaded onto narrow boats on the Montgomery Canal, which reached Llanymynech around 1790. The arrival of the canal meant that stone could be transported much more cheaply and easily than by the primitive roads of that time

When you walk the Offa's Dyke Path through Llanymynech you can still see plenty of evidence of the limestone industry. Beside the canal there is a special Heritage Area. (Look for the signs and the small car park off the main street, the A483). The star attraction here is a very large Hoffman Kiln, in which limestone could be burned continuously in a series of chambers. Above the village, the path goes up through the quarries, climbing part of the way on the surface of one of the old inclines – you'll see grooves in the rock of the path, cut by the winding cables. At the top, a stile marks the England/Wales border, and beyond are the tumble-down remains of the winding house.

In spring the inclined plane is lined with primroses, and later in the year white tresses of the wild clematis, 'old man's beard', can be seen draped over the trees and shrubs all around.

Hoffman Kiln chimney

Nesting swan, Montgomery Canal at Llanymynech

A signpost to stand the test of time and weather

Summer on the Severn

From Llanymynech Hill there are sweeping views back across the floodplains of the rivers Severn and Vyrnwy, towards the Breidden Hills. A long reach of the Severn is visible here, looking upstream towards Welshpool and down to Shrewsbury. Here and there the rivers catch the sun among the trees and fields; more so in winter, when whole fields may be under water.

Eventually the path emerges from the quarries onto a golf course on the top of the hill. Here can be seen the first substantial piece of Offa's Dyke since Four Crosses. This part of the path tends to get overgrown with bracken, which in the normal run of events would simply be cut back, but this particular area of bracken provides an important habitat for rare butterflies, and has to be carefully managed.

Descending the northern side of Llanymynech Hill below Blodwell Rock, you come to Porth-y-waen. Here Margaret Worthington, who studied Offa's Dyke for many years with Dr David Hill of Manchester University, now runs a field centre. It is called Porth y Waen Study Centre and offers a range of non-residential short holiday archaeology courses.

Approaching the limestone hill of Moelydd, you pass through the small nature reserve of Jones's Rough, which is managed by the Shropshire Wildlife Trust. And just below the Rough is a cottage occupied by Doug Hughes, a retired teacher from Cheshire. Doug is a keen gardener and a very useful volunteer, who keeps an eye on both the nature reserve and National Trail.

The Offa's Dyke Path takes a rather tortuous route over Moelydd, winding this way and that on paths and tracks through bracken and scrub. At one time walkers used to go astray here regularly, a situation which was not helped by an Offa's Dyke Path sign which was loosely attached to a round steel pole, and turned in the wind. Some years ago now, I took a group from the Shropshire Conservation Volunteers up the hill to waymark the path properly. It seemed obvious to me that the solution to the problem of the rotating sign was to put up a proper timber fingerpost, firmly set in the ground. It did not take long to find out why this had not been done the first time. The soil on the summit of Moelydd is but a few inches deep, and beneath that is solid limestone bedrock. A crowbar

was called for. With its aid, two determined volunteers managed to get down about a foot and, I confess, we finished off the job with concrete.

Though you are in Shropshire here, there are plenty of descriptive Welsh place-names on which to practise the vocabulary you picked up down in Monmouthshire. Descending from Moelydd we pass the farm of Moelydd Uchaf (Upper Hill-tops), and a little further on Tŷ Canol (Middle House). On the other side of the valley and a little lower down is Tŷ Isa (Lower House). So as you descend, you have the words to go with it.

Making your way through Candy Woods, you will be briefly separated from the dyke again, but will soon rejoin it. From the mature woodland of Racecourse Wood you will eventually emerge onto **Oswestry Old Racecourse**.

Managed by Oswestry Borough Council, this public open space is a very popular spot with casual walkers. There's a car park here, a picnic site, and a viewpoint with a toposcope. From the grandstand there used to be fine views across to the Berwyn Mountains but sadly, these are fast disappearing behind a conifer plantation. A little to the north, at Carreg-y-big, you're back on Offa's Dyke. A disagreement with the landowner back in the early days of the National Trail means that you'll have to follow the road over Baker's Hill rather than the earthwork.

By a farm called Orseddwen the modern border between England and Wales rejoins the ancient one. For the next 2½ miles (4 km) Offa's Dyke is the border once more, England is to the right, Wales to the left. Prepare yourself for ups and downs! Carreg-y-big is 1,030 ft (314 m) above sea level, but a picturesque meandering track leads gradually downhill to Craignant. There you pass a pair of limekilns on the side of the path before climbing again. The dyke is then a plateau for about a mile, before there are several flights of steps (originally installed by the army) down into Nanteris dingle, and several more flights up the other side. Not long after this comes quite a steep descent into the Ceiriog valley at Bronygarth, with views across to Chirk Castle on the opposite side of the valley.

Primroses, Candy Woods

Racecourse Wood

Lime-loving plants

Old limestone workings often provide excellent habitat for wildlife and for wild flowers in particular. They offer a combination of lime-rich soils and relative tranquility, whether in busy urban areas or in intensively-farmed countryside. The Llanymynech quarries are a typical example. Both the Montgomeryshire Wildlife Trust and Shropshire Wildlife Trust manage nature reserves on Llanymynech Hill, by arrangement with the owners, LaFarge Aggregates. These reserves are home to many lime-loving plants as well as some rare butterflies.

There is something uplifting just in the names of some plants – **eyebright** (*Euphrasia nemorosa*) is one such. The tiny flowers, about 5mm across, are very aptly-named. Another to make you smile is the climbing **traveller's-joy** (*Clematis vitalba*). This wild version of the garden clematis is also known as old man's beard from the grey cascades of hairy plumes it produces when in seed.

Everyone loves an orchid, and the **early-purple orchid** (*Orchis mascula*) is a relatively common one. Here it is growing right on the edge of the National Trail, below Asterley Rocks, on Llanymynech Hill.

WILD CARROT

Though not particularly well-known, the wild carrot *Daucus carota* gives its name to a whole family of plants: the carrot family, or *umbelliferae*. The more common cow parsley and hogweed are both members of this family, and all three have the characteristic flat-topped, umbrella-shaped array of florets known as an *umbel*. Pictured here is a carrot plant in late summer. Flowering over, the umbel has closed up to form a miniature basket full of carrot seeds.

NAMES:
English: wild carrot
Latin: *Daucus carota*
Welsh: moronen y maes

*NATURE FILE * NATURE FILE * NATURE FILE*

NAMES:

English: eyebright	**Latin:** *Euphrasia officinalis*	**Welsh:** effros llygad siriol
English: traveller's-joy	**Latin:** *Clematis vitalba*	**Welsh:** barf yr hen ŵr
English: early-purple orchid	**Latin:** *Orchis mascula*	**Welsh:** tegeirian coch y gwanwyn

LATE SUMMER DELIGHTS

As a child I learned that my father, who had been in the Royal Artillery during the Second World War, was unable to hear the high-pitched sound of the **grasshopper**. A shame, since this gentle churring is surely the very essence of summer. The sound is generated by the grasshopper rapidly rubbing its hind legs against its abdomen. The technical term is stridulating; and when I was last on Llanymynech Hill, on a sunny day in early September, they were doing it everywhere.

I found these windfall apples under a solitary tree among the quarry waste tips on Llanymynech Hill. The tree may be a genuine wild **crab apple,** *Malus sylvestris,* but Richard Mabey reports that 'wilding' apple trees are much more common. These spring up in the wild from the seeds in discarded apple cores, and produce fruits of all shapes and sizes. So perhaps these apples are the offspring of a quarryman's lunch. Now can I find anyone to make me some crab apple and blackberry jelly?

NAMES: **English:** grasshopper   **Latin:** *Acrididae sp.*   **Welsh:** ceiliog rhedyn

Mel and Eric Robinson

Bridge over the river Ceiriog

The celebrated writer George Borrow stood on the bridge here 150 years ago, and wrote about it in his book, *Wild Wales*:

> I ordered some ale and bread-and-butter, and whilst our repast was being got ready John Jones and I went to the bridge. 'This bridge sir,' said John, 'is called Pont y Felin Castell, the bridge of the Castle Mill; the inn was formerly the mill of the castle, and is still called Melin y Castell. As soon as you are over the bridge you are in shire Amwythig, which the Saxons call Shropshire. A little way up on yon hill is Clawdd Offa or Offa's Dyke, built of old by the Brenin Offa in order to keep us poor Welsh within our bounds.' As we stood on the bridge I enquired of Jones the name of the brook which was running merrily beneath it. 'The Ceiriog, sir', said John.

Borrow's Inn, which had been a mill, is now Castle Mill Cottages, a row of three, in one of which Eric and Mel Robinson live. I knocked on their door one September evening to ask if they would mind posing for a photograph at the Ceiriog Bridge, and Mel showed me the way down to the river so that I could see the bridge from below. It is certainly a very much more impressive structure than one would know from walking over it.

Despite being quite a (self-taught) expert on both the Welsh language and Welsh literary traditions, Borrow was not aware then of the work of a contemporary poet, John Ceiriog Hughes, who published his first volume of poetry in 1860, just two years before Borrow's own *Wild Wales*. The young poet, known simply as Ceiriog, went on to write some of the best-loved poems in the Victorian era. The lyrics were recited and sung on concert platforms throughout Wales, and many songs, such as 'David of the White Rock', remain popular to this day.

DIGGING INTO HISTORY

Chirk Castle

Not the archetypal romantic Welsh castle, Chirk is nevertheless the real thing. It was built in the 14th Century by Roger Mortimer, who had helped Edward I to defeat Llywelyn, Prince of Wales. According to Trevor Rowley in *The Landscape of the Welsh Marches* Chirk was one of the six principal royal castles of the Welsh Marches during the later Middle Ages. In 1534 these castles were reported to be in a very poor state of repair, but today Chirk is fully habitable and has all the accoutrements, inside and out, of a stately home.

Bought by Sir Thomas Myddelton in 1595, Chirk Castle was twice besieged in the 17th century, once by Myddleton's son, who had lost it to the Royalists in the Civil War. The castle is now in the care of the National Trust but the Myddleton family lives locally still and owns much of the surrounding land, including parts crossed by the Offa's Dyke Path.

timewatch

1595

The castle at Chirk was sold for £5,000 pounds to Sir Thomas Myddelton. His descendants continue to live in part of the castle today.

1600

Edward Llwyd, scholar, naturalist and man of letters whose writings have been inspirational, was born in Oswestry. The Welsh-language natural history society is named after him: Cymdeithas Edward Llwyd. Their logo is the Snowdon lily, whose Latin name also commemorates the great man.

Lloydia serotina

1848

This was the last year of racing at Oswestry Racecourse outside the town. Horseracing began here in the early 1700s and parts of the 2-mile figure of eight track are still marked on the OS map, on either side of the B4580.

1862

George Borrow published the first edition of Wild Wales. This was so different from the other sober and factual chronicles of walks through Wales that it proved far too original for many Victorian readers. The ostentatious, boisterous and tale-weaving Borrow has been popular ever since.

Thomas Telford 1757-1834

You cannot miss the works of Thomas Telford when you walk the northern half of the Offa's Dyke Path.

Telford was the great pioneer of civil engineering, who for much of his career was based in Shropshire, where he was County Surveyor of Public Works. He designed and built bridges, canals, churches, and roads. The Montgomeryshire branch of his Shropshire Union Canal and the flood defences by the river Severn, which he is believed to have worked on, have already been noted. This part of the journey ends at the side of his London to Holyhead Road, and the next sets out along his Llangollen Canal.

Possibly Telford's two most famous works are the Pont Cysyllte Aquedect – which is featured in the next chapter – and the London to Holyhead Road, now known as the A5. Holyhead is directly across the Irish Sea from Dublin, and has for centuries been a major port for embarkation for Ireland. So before the arrival of the railways, the London to Holyhead road was of considerable strategic importance. To make a continuous route some major engineering works were required, including the construction of a new road through the

mountains of Snowdonia and a suspension bridge over the Menai Strait, completed in 1826. Both are still in use 180 years later, though the bridge was strengthened in the twentieth century. But as well as grand works of engineering, Telford had an eye for fine detail. He designed the toll houses and even the milestones which marked out the route to Holyhead. One of each can be seen beside the A5 in Llangollen today.

Borrow had just walked down the hill from Chirk Castle, which he described as 'a mansion ancient and beautiful, and abounding with all kinds of agreeable and romantic associations'.

The castle and gardens are now in the care of the National Trust, and if you are here in the summer you have the opportunity to retrace Borrow's steps. The official route of the Offa's Dyke Path skirts round the Chirk estate to the west but, during the months when the castle is open walkers are allowed to follow the dyke uphill through the park to the Home Farm, where you can obtain a ticket to see the house and gardens. There is, of course, a National Trust tearoom, and if you are member (and so do not have to pay for admission), you might like to just nip into the courtyard for a pot of Earl Grey and slice of sponge cake. That's what I do.

Whether or not you stop for tea, you can spot the earthwork from the National Trust car park, as it heads off toward the ornamental lake. It is in a very much degraded state here, and amounts to no more than a slight rise in the ground. But soon it disappears from sight entirely, passing right through the middle of the lake, to emerge again in a wood on the far side. This part of the park is still in private hands, but I am told that if you know what you are doing (and have enough faith) it is possible to walk across the lake on the crest of the dyke, which is only *just* below the water.

If you choose to visit Chirk Castle by road, pause to admire the extraordinary wrought iron gates, which date from 1719.

Official and 'permissive' routes of the National Trail meet again at Tyn-y-groes and then follow lanes and paths downhill to meet the dyke again at Thomas Telford's famous London to Holyhead road, the A5. Please take great care here. This is still one of the busiest roads into north Wales, and a stile over a stone wall brings you down on the very edge of the tarmac.

Chirk Castle gardens

Gates to the Chirk estate

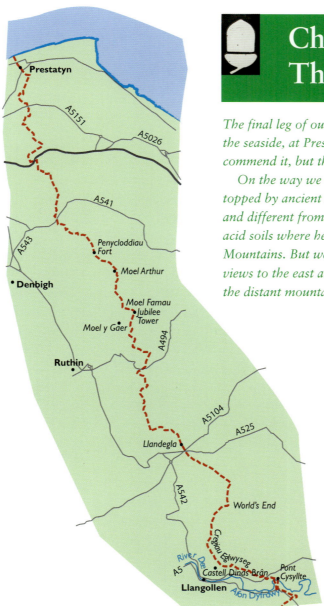

Chapter VIII :
The Clwydian Hills

The final leg of our journey along the Offa's Dyke Path takes us to the seaside, at Prestatyn, where architecture may not have much to commend it, but the ice-cream is good.

On the way we traverse the open hills of the Clwydian range, topped by ancient hill-forts. The landscape here is quite distinctive, and different from most that we have seen so far. We are back on acid soils where heather and bilberry grow, as they did in the Black Mountains. But we are well into north Wales now, so that the views to the east are of the Cheshire plain, and to the west we see the distant mountains of Snowdonia.

In the Dee valley, the Offa's Dyke Path again divides, and the walker has a choice of routes. This time the lower route takes a tarmac road (the B5434) down to the old stone bridge over the Dee, while the upper route takes in an ancient monument of a unique kind. This is the famous **Pont Cysyllte aqueduct**, which carries the Llangollen Canal across the valley, 121 feet (36 m) above the river Dee. If you are not good with heights I recommend the road. Crossing the aqueduct from the south you have good solid iron railings to your right, but only the canal, which runs in a cast-iron trough, to your left. (Note how the trough is constructed in a series of arches, each made up of individually-shaped tapered iron plates, bolted edge-to-edge.) I often used to wonder what it must be like to cross in a boat, for the channel is very narrow, and there is no parapet at all on the far side. One day I decided to find out. I hitched a lift on the good ship *Furness Railway No. 35*, and perched in the bow with my camera. Although I'm not particularly worried by heights, I decided *not* to lean over the side but, instead, hold my camera out at arm's length, pointing down. The result was quite interesting and confirmed that it is indeed a long way down to the river below.

Each of the Dee crossings offers a very good view of the other, and if you want to sample both you can make a circular walk of about one mile by crossing one and returning on the other. Once again I discovered that George Borrow has been here before us, taking the same walk in the 1850s:

> 'This is the Pont y Cysswllt, sir' said my guide; 'it's the finest bridge in the world, and no wonder, if what the common people say be true, namely that every stone cost a golden sovereign.' We went along it; the height was awful. My guide, though he had been a mountain shepherd, confessed that he was somewhat afraid. 'It gives me the pendro, sir,' said he, 'to look down.' I too felt somewhat dizzy, as I looked over the parapet in to the glen. The canal which this mighty bridge carries across the gulf is about nine feet wide, and occupies about two-thirds of the width of the bridge and the entire western side. The footway is

Sign on the Llangollen Canal

Pont Cysyllte aqueduct over the river Dee

Narrow boat decked out for summer

Castell Dinas Brân

towards the east. From about the middle of the bridge there is a fine view of the forges on the Cefn Bach, and also of a huge hill near it called the Cefn Mawr. We reached the termination, and presently crossing the canal by a little wooden bridge we came to a village. My guide then said 'If you please, sir, we will return by the old bridge, which leads across the Dee in the bottom of the vale.' He then led me by a romantic road to a bridge on the west of the aqueduct and far below. It seemed very ancient. 'This is the old bridge, sir,' said my guide; 'it was built a hundred years before the Pont y Cysswllt was dreamt of.'

Whichever way you choose to cross the river Dee you will find yourself on the towpath of the Llangollen Canal again shortly afterwards. If you want to see Llangollen at close quarters you could choose to leave the National Trail for a while and follow the canal westward. If not, you will still have views across the Dee valley to the town from the Panorama Walk, after you climb through Trevor Hall Wood. From the Panorama Walk our route follows the contours on a narrow tarmac road, with the limestone crags of Trevor Rocks on the right, and to our left, Castell Dinas Brân crowning the summit of a steep conical hill. According to some the name is supposed to signify 'Crow Castle' but historian Frank Price Jones, author of *Crwydro Dwyrain Dinbych* (Exploring East Denbighshire) insists that such an interpretation is inexcusable. Although less dramatic, George Burrow's translation is nearer the mark: 'the castle of Bran or Brennus, or the castle above the Brân, a brook which flows at its feet.'

Rooting about for some fossils to photograph at Trevor Rocks one afternoon, I heard raucous laughter. Sarah Lean and Gemma Home Roberts were leaning against a rock-face having quite a noisy picnic. They were out for the day from Shrewsbury for a bit of climbing along with Karo, their elderly and slightly deaf dog. When I returned that way later they had got down (or is that up?) to serious business, ropes and all. Sarah and Gemma, that is. Karo was watching from a safe distance.

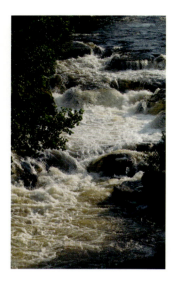

Llangollen is possibly the most widely-known town in Wales, thanks to its famous International Eisteddfod. It is also on the A5, the traditional route into north Wales for generations of holidaymakers from England, so it is a town accustomed to catering for visitors. If you decide to go there you will find not just an abundance of Welsh memorabilia, but also a steam railway and some scenic waterfalls on the river Dee. At the church of St Collen there is a memorial to Lady Eleanor Butler and her 'companion', Sarah Ponsonby, together known as the Ladies of Llangollen.

Somewhere beyond Castell Dinas Brân, Trevor Rocks merge into Creigiau Eglwyseg, then at Rock Farm we leave the road and come to what is probably the most spectacular part of the whole National Trail. The path traverses steep limestone screes on its way to the head of the valley of the Eglwyseg river, the apocalyptically-named World's End, below the shadows of Craig y Cythraul, the devil's rock! This is another rich area for wildlife, where I have seen the day-flying little owl *Athene noctua*; I am fairly confident there will be peregrines, *Falco peregrinus*, here too.

If your world does not end at World's End you will soon find yourself crossing the heather moorland of Cyrn y Brain on a protective boardwalk. There are grouse here. Listen out for their low-pitched rhythmic call, which my bird book describes as 'kok-kok-kok'. I wish I could come up with a better description, but all I can add is that you *may* be reminded of the sound of a car with a flat battery, failing to start. From the moorland we descend through a large area of forestry toward the village of Llandegla, where, of course, stands the church of St Tegla.

Soon after Llandegla begins the climb into the hills of the Clwydian Range, which will take us all the way to Prestatyn. The landscape here is quite distinctive; as on Hatterrall Ridge, the soil is acid and heather thrives. There is some commercial forestry in these hills, but the tops are mostly treeless, and we stay at a fairly high altitude for most of the route, dropping occasionally to a 'bwlch' between summits.

River Dee at Llangollen

World's End

Wildlife on Every Side

The sheer variety of wildlife to be enjoyed from the Offa's Dyke Path is not to be underestimated. Where there is conifer plantation on one side and open moorland on the other, there is scope for many kinds of small mammals, birds and insects. Heather in full bloom is an obvious attraction to bees and butterflies such as the red admiral and the speckled wood butterfly.

NAMES: **English**: Speckled wood butterfly
Latin: *Pararge aegeria*
Welsh: Brith y coed

As for birds, look out for little gold crests and coal-tits. But if it's spring, be ready for black grouse strutting out from beneath the trees, eager to mate on the moorland or, indeed, on the path itself. They also feed on the cotton grass abundant on open moorland, for the seedheads are nutritious.

NAMES: **English**: black grouse **Latin**: *Tetrao tetrix*
Welsh: grugiar

GOLDCREST

Conifers make a good home for goldcrests, those tiny, busy birds that weigh only a few ounces. Like all small birds and mammals, they have to feed constantly and their chief prey is insects and spiders, so ivy-covered trees and conifer plantations offer considerable sustenance. Goldcrests are a fairly common breeding bird in Wales, and the winter population is greatly augmented by immigrants from the far north. Iolo Williams considers it 'yet another of nature's many miracles . . . that our smallest bird can fly such long distances over water'.

NAMES:
English: goldcrest
Latin: *Regulus regulus*
Welsh: eurben

NATURE FILE * NATURE FILE * NATURE FILE *

TREVOR ROCKS

Trevor Rocks are popular with fossil hunters for there are tantalising imprints in these limestone outcrops which even an amateur geologist will enjoy. It is also a good place for climbers if you like your ascents and descents to be manageable without too much equipment. For botanists, the crowning glory of this place has to be the carline thistle in late summer. Growing right at the base of rocks dotted around the hillside, these stemless specimens are like bursts of sunshine.

NAMES: **English:** stemless carline thistle   **Latin:** *Carlina acaulis*   **Welsh:** ysgallen y calch
(lit. lime thistle)

Fiona Gale

View from Moel Arthur

At 1,817 feet (554 m) **Moel Famau** is the highest summit of the Clwydian range. On a clear day you can see it from the centre of Liverpool, and it is a traditional destination for a Bank Holiday outing for Merseysiders. In 1995 our automatic people-counter by the car park below the hilltop counted 100,000 people heading off in the direction of the Jubilee Tower, which marks the summit. This is probably the busiest section of the Offa's Dyke Path. Of course, if you can see Moel Famau from Liverpool it follows that you can see Liverpool, and much else besides, from Moel Famau.

About 1¾ miles north of Moel Famau the path descends steeply to a small car park where I met Fiona Gale late one September afternoon. Fiona has been County Archaeologist for Denbighshire since 1996 and has been working recently on the Heather and Hill-forts project, in which a range of organisations have come together to conserve and restore the archaeology and ecology of six hill-forts in this part of Wales. Three of them – Foel Fenlli, Moel Arthur and Penycloddiau – are on the Offa's Dyke Path, and Moel y Gaer (Llanbedr) is close by.

Fiona and I were here to take a look at the **Moel Arthur** fort, so from the car park we set off north along the Offa's Dyke Path, which skirts round the east side of the hill, passing a rather fine slate waymark 'post' with carved direction arrows. Here we turned off the National Trail to walk up to the fort itself and do a circuit of the ramparts. The air was clear, but it was late afternoon and overcast, not ideal conditions for photography. I was taking some pictures of Fiona when suddenly the sun broke through onto a patch of fields in the vale below so I hared off to find a better vantage point. Some women might be offended by this kind of behaviour, but Fiona came immediately to admire the view. Strange to think that some 2,000 years ago, people at this hill-fort would have looked out from the same vantage point, though certainly not down on the pattern of hedges, fields and farms we see today.

As we descended to the car park again, Fiona casually remarked, pointing to a heap of stones, 'Oh, did you know that was an old gold mine?' But before you rush up there with your pick and shovel I should point out that they didn't find much gold there, so it was abandoned long ago.

DIGGING INTO HISTORY

The Jubilee Tower

Moel Famau is the highest mountain of the Clwydian Range, but its prominence is enhanced by the Jubilee Tower which crowns the summit. This gives the hill a distinctive outline, which is instantly recognisable from all points of the compass.

The tower we see today is merely the base of what was originally a 150ft (46m) obelisk, which collapsed in 1862.

The construction of the tower began in 1810, and the Jubilee in its name was that of King George III. This was the George who shortly afterwards went mad and was replaced by his son the Prince Regent, who gave us London's Regent's Park and the architectural term 'Regency'.

The tower's remains now offer a convenient objective for a flagging walker, and, once the objective is attained, a good viewpoint and perhaps some shelter from the wind for a restful picnic.

c. 800

The Pillar of Eliseg was built in honour of Elisedd ap Gwylog – it seems that the carver made an error when words were inscribed on the stone. Originally a cross, it gives its name to Valle Crucis, valley of the cross, but it was much defaced by Cromwell's troops in the seventeenth century. When it was re-erected in 1779, the mound on which it stands was opened: it contained a skeleton buried in a stone cist, with a silver coin enclosed.

1848

The Chester and Holyhead railway reached the north Wales coast, bringing holidaymakers from cities in the north of England to enjoy the seaside – and views such as this one of the Great Orme, near Llandudno, from Prestatyn.

1947

The first International Eisteddfod was held at Llangollen, to help heal the wounds of the Second World War. In 2004, Terry Waite nominated the Eisteddfod for a Nobel Peace Prize.

1900

Sleepers were laid on the damaged peat areas of Cyrn y Brain to combat erosion, and have been very successful.

SLATE AROUND LLANGOLLEN

One of the principal cargoes on the narrow boats crossing Pont Cysyllte would have been slate from the numerous quarries around Llangollen.

Slate is a metamorphic rock which, because it is non-porous, and can be readily split into very thin sheets, makes an ideal roofing material. It is also easily sawn and cut to a variety of sizes.

In the eighteenth and nineteenth century slate quarrying was an important industry around Llangollen, though not on the scale of quarrying elsewhere in north Wales. Much of the slate from the Llangollen area was used as slab slate for flooring, tanks, gravestones and even billiard tables. The arrival of canals, and later railways, enabled Welsh slate to be exported all over Britain and beyond. It became the standard roofing material of Britain's Victorian cities, replacing 'vernacular' materials such as clay tiles or thatch. George Borrow in *Wild Wales* reports a conversation with a boatman who took slates from Llangollen to Paddington (London) by canal, a journey which took three weeks.

In the twentieth century, Welsh slate was gradually superseded by concrete roof tiles, and many of the quarries have long since closed. Today, if you want to repair a slate roof, you will probably find yourself buying imports from Spain. But the remains of the Llangollen slate industry can still be seen dotted about the landscape, including tips of waste slate alongside the A542 as it climbs the Horseshoe Pass, north of the town.

What's on your roof?

The very next summit after Moel Arthur is **Penycloddiau**. The fort here is very much larger than on Moel Arthur: the National Trail enters the fort via the southern rampart and proceeds over half a mile before leaving again at the northern end. I was last on Penycloddiau on a fine day in August. The sun shone, heather bloomed and swallows flew low over the ramparts in a gentle breeze. Through the haze I could just pick out the Peckforton Hills and a flare on the refineries at Stanlow, both in Cheshire. Snowdonia was just visible too.

As I lay full length in the heather, photographing the tiny purple flowers, I heard voices and raised my head to see Diane Burns and Shirley Johnson walking by – old friends from Wallasey and Birkenhead, respectively, out for a day's walking together. I had been planning to visit Moel Famau later to find some Merseysiders but here they were on Penycloddiau!

After two weeks travelling in King Offa's footsteps through the bucolic tranquility of the borders, **Prestatyn** may come as a bit of a shock. True it is not quite Blackpool, but it is certainly a long way from Montgomery: you will not find much genteel Georgian architecture here. Plenty of ice-cream though, a fact which Iolo and Tessa made the most of when they were filming here.

Prestatyn Town Council is fiercely proud of their connection with Offa's Dyke, even though the dyke is not to be found in the town, and there is no hard archaeological evidence to suggest that it ever was. However, Sir Cyril Fox, whose 1953 magnum opus *Offa's Dyke* is still the most authoritative published work on the subject, did endorse the view that Prestatyn was the *most likely* terminus of the earthwork in Offa's time. Presumably this, along with the presence of a convenient railway station, was the reason that the Offa's Dyke Path was directed here when maps of the route were laid out in the 1950s.

Anyway, whatever the reasons, and whatever you make of the wind-farms just off the coast, Prestatyn is where our journey ends. So whether you celebrate with an ice-cream, as Iolo and Tessa did, or take tea outside the Nova Centre like me, pause to savour your achievement. Look out to sea and make a resolution to return – to marvel again at the glories of Offa's Dyke.

Diane and Shirley among the heather

View from Penycloddiau

ACKNOWLEDGEMENTS

My list of thanks must be headed with mention of Mrs Rebe Brick, who has been a good friend and supportive colleague to me for 17 years. Rebe retires from her post as Manager of the Offa's Dyke Centre in Knighton just as this book goes to press. Thank you, Rebe.

I would also like to acknowledge the five women without whom this book would not have happened – Enid Davies, Sarah Duggan, Mairwen Jones, Zarine Katrak and Mariel Thomas.

For help with research and photograph captions, my thanks go to: Barbara Atkins, Ian Bapty, Andrew Blake, Mark Bristow, Peter Dorling, Dave Drewett, Fiona Gale, Emma Heggarty, Helen Jones, Marianne Jones, Ben Moss, Lucy MacFarlane, Nancy Millington, Glyn Owens, George Peterken, Celia Richardson, Mike Scruby, Sandra Sharp, David Shiel, Paula Slack and Mark Walters.

And for agreeing to be photographed, whether they got into the book or not: Ian Bapty, Willem and Hilde Bogtstra, Alan Bridgewater, Bob and Gaynor Bright, Rob Burn, Diane Burns, the Butlin Family of Reading, David and Ruth Clarke, Anne Mary Davies, Gareth Davies, Corinne Donaldson, Tessa Dunlop, Carol Ferris and Richard Griffiths, Holly George, Alice Goldstone and Gary Cowell, Andy Hazell, Shirley Johnson, Nigel Jones, Helen Karllson, Zarine Katrak, Matt Kemp, Alex Lewis, Barry Lewis, Sally Lewis, Sam Llewelyn, Sarah Marshall, Peter Mayes, Egmont Mooij, Russell Odell, Bert Payne, Sandra Pemberton, Joanna Phillips, Dave Potter, Haydn Price, Jill Ranford, Oliver Ridgewell, Eric and Mel Robinson, Peter Robinson, Ruth Rourke, Fred Salt, Lewis Saunders, Mike Scruby, Claire Smith, Jason Stanton, Anne Sutton, Rob and Kitty Thomson, John and Di Walton, Alastair and Judy Watt, Clare Willets, Alan Williams, Hannah Williams, Iolo Williams and Francis Choo Yin.

I am grateful to Mark Thackara at Olympus Optical UK for the loan of a very nice 7-14mm super-wide-angle lens, and to Iolo Williams for his enthusiasm and his foreword. And finally, for keeping me sane long enough to become an author, thank you to my GP, Dr Anthony Lempert.

JS

The author and publishers gratefully acknowledge permission granted by Powys County Council, the Countryside Council for Wales and Natural England to reproduce photographs by Jim Saunders which are part of their archives.